Australian Women Can Walk

Gap Year 1979

India, Sri Lanka, and Nepal

Veronica Caven Aldous

Australian Women Can Walk
Gap Year 1979
India, Sri Lanka and Nepal

Published through IngramSpark

Copyright ©2021 by Veronica Caven Aldous

ISBN: 978-0-6451693-0-0 (Paperback Edition)
ISBN: 978-0-6451693-1-7 (eBook Edition)

No part of this publication may be reproduced, stored in a retrieval system, or transmitted in any form or by any means electronic, mechanical, photocopying, recording, or otherwise, without the written permission of the author or publisher.

Contents

Part 1: Melbourne, Kuala Lumpur, Calcutta, Srinagar and Trekking 1

Favourable Winds to Kuala Lumpur 3
Calcutta 6
A Sunday in Calcutta 8
Travel Plans 10
We Talked About Yoga 12
Our Last Day in Calcutta 14
Calcutta to Kashmir 17
We Arrived in Srinagar 18
Dal Lake, Srinagar 22
The New Houseboat Hull 28
More Time on the Houseboat 37
Adrian Went to London While We Went to Yusmarg ... 43
Back on the Houseboat 44
Shikara Trek 47
New Travellers 53
Planning a Trek, Drawing, a Mosque Visit, and a Wedding 57
Trek to the Kolahoi Glacier 60
Heading South 73
Yusmarg and Back in Srinagar 77
I Left Kashmir But Ryan Stayed 82

Part 2: South into India, Sri Lanka and Back to India 85

    Delhi, Agra, Bombay, Ajanta and Ellora 87
    Not Goa, then Ooty, Bangalore, and Mysore 92
    Cochin and Trivandrum 94
    Kanyakumari 98
    Madurai 102
    Colombo Then Kandy 104
    Colombo and Hikkaduwa 106
    Tiruchirappalli, Madras, Pondicherry, Puri 110
    How to Get on a Bus 115
    Bus Stop 117
    Heaven in a Field 119
    Monkeys on a Train 121
    The Bikers 123
    Night Trains 124
    Bananas 125

Part 3: Calcutta to Nepal, Trekking, Some Northern Indian Cities, and Bangkok to Melbourne 127

    Calcutta Again 129
    Headed North 132
    Nepal 134
    Kathmandu 137
    Bhaktapur 139
    To Pokhara 142
    Flew Back to Kathmandu to Extend My Visa 147
    Nagarkot 154
    Back to Pokhara On My Own 164
    Poon Hill Trek 168
    Back to Pokhara 194

Back to Kathmandu 196
Kathmandu 198
More Kathmandu 200
Slept with a Rat 212
Flew to Patna, Bus to Varanasi and Met Ryan Again ... 213
Gaya and Bodh Gaya 216
Calcutta for the Third Time and Ryan Headed Home .. 219
To Laksar 220
Cracked Heads at Laksar Station 221
Rishikesh 223
Delhi 231
Jaipur 232
Back to Delhi 233
Bangkok 235
Melbourne 236
And Then 237

PART 1

Melbourne, Kuala Lumpur, Calcutta, Srinagar and Trekking

Favourable Winds to Kuala Lumpur

"We had favourable winds," the pilot announced as we landed in Kuala Lumpur forty-five minutes ahead of schedule after slowly circling the peninsula of Malaysia. Walking towards the exits and out of the airport my mind was reeling. *Here we go.* I played at being unconcerned. Faking it that I was cool and calm. I had to back myself. I often pretended I was in control and okay when I wasn't, but this scene of mayhem at the airport pushed me even further out of my comfort zone.

I was with Ryan, a friend from art school, and his friend Adrian, who I had known for a while too. Ryan was shocked when we met at the check-in desk at Melbourne airport. I looked very different. I had changed my appearance as a safety strategy to look neutral. It was a given that women had to be careful backpacking at home or overseas.

I had my hair cut short, didn't wear make-up or jewellery and wore a simple shirt with two pockets on the front to camouflage my breasts, and long cotton trousers. I only took a small backpack and hid a pouch in my trousers with my passport and traveller cheques. The air steward and customs officer at Melbourne airport both called me "sir" and questioned if I was male or female, saying, "you have changed" when looking at the longhaired girl in my passport photo. So it had worked.

Our very loose plan was to travel to Europe, and this was our first step. We might go overland or fly over some countries. Was it Australian to think we would work it out as we went along? Or was it being young? I had some kind of confidence. I was still training as a one hundred metres sprinter, could run it in twelve seconds, and hoped I was able to get away if challenged.

The exits here at the K.L. airport were guarded, but open to show the crowds of people outside. People were loudly spruiking for various hotels and cab services and really wanted your business.

We burst out through this threshold from the cool air-conditioning, throwing ourselves into the extreme humidity. I immediately felt like I was melting. There was chaotic noise, a great deal of jostling and no one trying to create any order. I smelt plane fumes, heavily polluted, mouldy air, and human sweat.

A little stupefied, we acted deliberately and calmly as we walked to a large shuttle bus for the South East Asian Hotel, as if we had done it all before. I did not look back into the airport from where we had come in case the fear and adrenalin overtaking me as I walked might throw off my forward momentum.

We checked in on the 8th of May. We dropped our bags and then wandered for hours in the food stalls around the hotel in China Town. We ate crisp deep-fried curried potato puffs and coconut balls that had a covering of sesame seeds. I had never tasted anything like them. They were deliciously spiced and aromatic. I was used to eating more plain food. We soaked in the smells of frying oil, the hustle and bustle, and the sights and sounds of people living busy lives.

There was an ambient din of market noises and cacophony of peoples' voices spruiking. There was the ubiquitous odour of pollution and the pandemonium of sounds from the traffic.

The locals were well covered with multi-coloured clothes, long sleeved tops to their knees and trousers underneath as well. Many women had headscarves. There were women in vibrant intricately embroidered and coloured pantsuits or saris wearing gold jewellery. I felt completely absorbed in this new environment. Some were mothers and their children wore bright dresses or shorts with summer shirts. There were men in suits with briefcases and others in loose white clothes.

Could I live in Asia? Would I find something that might keep me here? Could I work here? Could I cope with this crush of population? I hoped this trip would ultimately change my life. At the airport just before we boarded our plane, Dad had said to me "give me twenty-four hours and I'll be there to walk you down the aisle anywhere." He clearly thought I might not come back.

At home I lived in a quiet eastern suburb of Melbourne. It was 1979, The White Australia policy ended in 1966 but the Racial Discrimination Act in 1975 was really needed to develop multiculturalism in Australia. We were underpopulated. Two years ago I had backpacked in Europe where the density of people had not overwhelmed me. The streets weren't crowded like this. The capital city of Malaysia felt like a sea of humanity. The *favourable winds* had swept us way out into the ocean. I felt alive and ready for more.

My heart was somersaulting, stimulated by the diversity and crush of people as I soaked in this new environment. I started to see more detail in the sea of faces. Some of the children in the streets looked saintly yet tough, with rugged faces. Looking into faces was stunningly stimulating. It seemed to be about survival above all in the marketplace. At times it was all too loud. I had no idea how to act so I stayed calm, tried not to panic, and treaded water.

There were children in the market sitting on wooden boxes writing in their exercise books. I had learnt very little about Australia's neighbouring countries. At school I had given up history when quite young, as it seemed like rubbish, either watered down or made up.

My two companions and I did not give each other much attention. We were present as conduits for each other. We glided around as a trio of curiosity, needing each other for momentum of movement, which bolstered our individual sense of bravery and safety. From time to time we would point out things with a nod, grunt, word, or nudge. In the crush we were often physically connected. I felt close with Ryan and Adrian. I felt our friendship. I thought they were also very happy exploring but at times did I see glimpses of discomfort, frustration, and a little panic in their eyes? Did I also look like that?

Calcutta

WE FLEW TO Calcutta next where the sun was ever-present. The vast sky and massive horizon surrounded and dominated the cityscape. Middle-distant views of large parks floated behind everything, even in the densely built up areas. People were sleeping in public places. There was dust in the air, heavy and thick. There were animals everywhere: monkeys, cows, dogs, and bats. Even though I found this intensely busy city stimulating I began to feel the world would very quickly become over populated.

We stayed in a family room at the Salvation Army Red Shield Guest House. It was really hot. Air-conditioning was ineffectual. We filled our bottles with boiled or filtered water provided there. We showered several times a day. It was forty-two degrees every day. Calcutta had thirteen million residents in the city and Australia had thirteen million in the whole country. I felt alive and it felt good to be travelling.

We had three single beds in a row with light blue cotton blankets. We laid the blankets on the floor in the tiny remaining space to do yoga. I was doing Transcendental Meditation (T.M.) so I sat on my bed after just a few minutes of yoga that I had learnt on a T.M. weekend. Friends at art school had told me to learn T.M. as I had a bad back from my athletics and I eventually did after going to three introductory talks, as I was quite sceptical. It was simple, no fuss, portable, and had fixed my anxiety and bad back. It made me happy.

I think Ryan and Adrian thought I was a bit lazy just sitting there on the bed with my eyes closed. They did an hour of yoga, explaining that the twisting activated certain nerve centres that affected particular organs so it was like an internal massage.

We ate veggie patties at the café there while we worked out what else we liked. We were vegetarian. I also thought not eating meat might keep me well in foreign places.

We visited the AUS, or Student Travel Office, further down the same street as our guest house. The manager was a tall man named J. D. Kapoor. He wore a red turban and was often in a white cotton singlet and lungi. He told us that he was there to help us at any time and that we should not smoke, drink, or take drugs.

One afternoon we were sitting in the big lounge room at the guest house under three steadily rotating large ceiling fans. Ryan was very intense at times so I avoided discussing anything too deeply with him, as he would flare up a bit. He made a statement about yoga and looked to see if I challenged it. I did not like debating so was evasive. Adrian was a lot more fun, very well read and an amazing intellect. I would have liked more time hanging out with Adrian on my own. They were close friends so often I felt a little excluded from their conversations. I did really enjoy their company though. I found them both attractive too but did not feel they were interested in me, which was good. It kept things simple.

We spoke with a girl called Parvati, from Madras, who was studying English and optometry. She gave us a sweet and we talked for a long time.

At about 7 p.m. we went with her to buy some yoghurt and cheap ripe or spoilt fruit from the markets. She wanted to use it to make us all fruit lassi. I paid for the fruit and she would show us how to make it, as it was new to us. She told me to eat the freshly made yoghurt in each new town to get the local gut bugs.

When we returned, Parvati went into the ladies' dorm to make the drinks. I could go in with her but not the guys. She had a small altar near her bed with a picture of Ganesh, her

Guru and a framed triptych of deities, next to a small white statue of a temple. In front of these were a lot of small bits and pieces, used incense sticks, lychees, bananas, and some old food that had been sitting there for a while. There was also a Bengali scripture that she used to recite to bless everything on the altar. Nearby there was a cardboard box of cut up dried leaves, petals and an apple.

With a small knife she peeled and seeded all the quite soft mangoes. She worked the fruit into a paste with her fingers then added some yoghurt, very grainy sugar and water to the jug. She poured the mixture into a cup, and then back again into the jug repeatedly, which made the lassi smooth.

I thought she was a very sweet person but she had some kind of strength you only get from a tough life on your own. My Australian friends and I had worked in various shops to easily save up our travelling money. We lived with our families. It was harder to earn and save money for Parvati as there were so many people looking for jobs in India and the wages were extremely low. I felt quite *soft*, privileged and middle class when with her.

When the lassi was ready, we all sat to drink it, with the light off in the shadows, on a bench outside the ladies' dorm, as it was cooler. It was so sweet and delicious.

A Sunday in Calcutta

THE NEXT MORNING was a Sunday and we were to go to the nearby Hindu Temple with Parvati, but she did not arrive. She could not find our room we later found out. While looking for her I met a Burmese girl in the ladies' dorm called Elizabeth. She took us instead to St. Paul's Anglican Cathedral, a large, white, Gothic church. It was comfortably full with people. It was near the Victoria Memorial Hall and extensive gardens next to the river.

Inside the church on a pew I found a prayer book. I had grown up a Catholic so was quite comfortable being there. It felt familiar and was relaxing, unleashing waves of childhood nostalgia. Inside the cover of this prayer book, I read that this was a high Protestant church with affiliated churches in Burma, Indonesia, India, Nepal, Afghanistan, Sri Lanka and more.

Elizabeth told us many things that day while we sat in the gardens outside the church. She worked for a British company in Calcutta and earned 2,000 rupees per month, about 250 dollars, so eight rupees per dollar. At the moment she was ill and on a pension of 500 rupees per month, about sixty dollars. I wondered what illness she had but she did not offer to explain. She recommended we visit a place on the coast south of Calcutta called Puri.

Walking away from the church along the long esplanades running next to the gardens and back to Sudder Street, we passed an Indian wedding procession of about one hundred people. Strangely, they all seemed serious or even angry. I did not engage with anyone, as I didn't know how to read the event.

When we returned to our room, I meditated, falling into a very deep sleep. As I woke I took some really relaxed deep breaths. Talking with Elizabeth about her everyday life here had given me a sense of normality in a strange place. It took the edge off my anxiety that I hadn't realised I had. The crush of population and encountering the unknown at every moment of every day had been making me quite anxious, mentally and physically. I hadn't quite had a panic attack, but perhaps it was building. My romance of the new had given way to the need for something familiar. I needed to feel safe. Later that day I noticed I had more confidence to resist becoming anxious when talking with strangers in the hotel and outside.

We went for a walk that afternoon and this time there were not many beggars in the street but men in smart slacks and shirts and women in elegant saris. The market was closed. So this was a taste of Sundays in Calcutta. It felt like a respite.

We met up with Andrew, a friend of Ryan's, who he knew from their yoga classes in Melbourne. He cooked at a bakery back home and had an interest in food wherever he travelled. We celebrated being there with a night eating South Indian dosas, another new food for us.

Travel Plans

THE NEXT DAY we decided to buy train tickets to Puri to get away from the heat. We walked along the Esplanade to the Eastern Ticket Office where there was a huge queue of people lined up along the street. Too hot to wait, we returned to our guest house, showered, rested, and drank water. We spent most of the day trying to deal with the heat; either hiding from it or recovering from being out in it. Each time I showered, I also washed my clothes and hung them in the bathroom to dry. They dried really quickly ready for the next change over. I was used to hot weather in Australia but this part of India was more unrelenting and humid.

We decided to go back to J.D. Kapoor at the AUS Office and ask his advice, and he offered a few recommendations. One idea was to try to go to Puri; another was to go to Bodh Gaya, the place where Buddha was enlightened under a Bodhi tree; and another was to take an express train all the way up to Srinagar in Kashmir. We could travel back down again in a few weeks when it was cooler. So we headed back again to the guest house to consider these options.

Emotionally we were frustrated and confused, missing the food and comforts of home. In the end we decided to travel by train over a couple of days to stay on a houseboat in Srinagar, Kashmir.

We went back to the crowded train office to buy tickets to Kashmir. Ryan was supporting me physically at times. I was nearly fainting. A fan flogged my loose-legged trousers and shirt. I was offered a seat and water. We sat in a queue with an older Sikh man who also was not operating well in the heat. We filled out a green form and had to show our passports. I also learnt that women could go to the front of the queue, which would help a lot next time.

As we left the office, my energy levels picked up. There was oxygen outside. We had our tickets! We strode out feeling triumphant, and slightly proud of ourselves. Ryan gave me a friendly hug to celebrate. Were we becoming closer?

We headed for the YMCA, where we had found a good café. While resting there in the cool lounge, full of rows of ceiling fans, a strong windstorm blew up. We stayed inside. I played chess against Ryan to pass the time. We didn't talk much. We looked at each other calmly and intently, as we hadn't done before. He won. He loved chess but I was ambivalent about it. I loved backgammon. We were getting used to spending time together. I was becoming less self-conscious. It was becoming easier. We watched fragments of ceiling plaster flake off the ceiling into the fans and spread out in the room as dust.

Many people were hiding out from the storm there in the YMCA lounge. From the balcony we could see that the wind had chased all of humanity away. The streets outside were deserted and only a red dusty haze filled the space.

We met Elizabeth again at the bar. We sat there for some time telling her about Australia, watching a red sunset, fantastic fork lightning, and dusty red wind settling due to light rain.

We Talked About Yoga

We walked briskly home to shower. I looked forward to doing my yoga and meditation. This always smoothed out the day and it was good to have some time to myself. I had been doing this twice a day for about eighteen months now, so it was a habit. It was simple and peaceful in the morning and evening. I laid my blue cotton blanket on the floor and began my routine.

The guys began interrupting me, gently questioning me about my yoga asanas. They did an hour of rigorous yoga learned from the large yoga school in Chapel Street, Prahran in Melbourne. Next came a barrage of questions from Ryan who clearly doubted the value of my practice. Adrian was gentler and described my asanas as subtle. It would be a shame for me to change them, as I loved them.

I talked about the translation of the Bhagavad Gita that I was reading. In it, Maharishi wrote about the *eightfold path* of Yoga. This understanding was that you could do all steps at the same time and even begin with meditation. Some translations use the term *eight-step* path of Yoga, which infers each technique comes one after the other, with meditation coming last. With T.M. you learn meditation first and it was the main thing. I was relieved when Ryan and Adrian decided to go out on to the balcony for peanuts and cordial, giving me some private time with less scrutiny.

I felt a slight rift between us, but I enjoyed their company; we spent a lot of time thinking and talking together. They also mentioned that they were trying to be celibate for a while so they didn't always want to be around me. They were happy to keep their own company sometimes. I didn't mind but I didn't believe Ryan. I felt we were becoming closer.

After meditating I felt very smooth emotionally and deeply rested. When talking with the guys again any issues seemed irrelevant to me. I had no reason to prove anything about my practice versus theirs. It was all the same to me. I loved this trip and these two guys and we would all get on fine.

Today I also felt we were getting over the culture shock of travelling in Asia. We were not so scared to do things and more readily went out and around the streets and shops. I felt more at ease with new people. The heat had abated after the storm and maybe we felt less overwhelmed because of that too. The storm was so beautiful, it felt like nature had visited us in the city, and afterward the air smelt clean and the light was much softer.

Ryan was talking about how the human race and natural environment would be able to survive. We all already felt that the world population was too much and we didn't want to have children to add to this.

Ryan was deep into the philosophy of yoga and we talked about books we had read recently. Adrian was very widely read and he worked in a bookshop in Melbourne. I had been reading about air, water, and basic elements in nature from a Chinese philosopher and also Yogi Ramacharaka. This yogi was actually William Walker Atkinson, an attorney, entrepreneur, publisher, writer, and occultist from Baltimore in the U.S.A. who was a pioneer in the New Thought movement of the early nineteenth century. One basic idea from him was that the mind was the basis for disease.

After that conversation I felt I was back in the mainstream of my *raison d'être* for this travel. I remembered how much I had got out of my earlier trip to Europe two years ago. I even thought to myself in French for a while, as I remembered Paris. It helped me to seize upon the joy of being in a foreign place. It was so stimulating, at times frightening, and I enjoyed wide-reaching conversation with friends or strangers. I didn't want to compare India with Europe but be open to whatever came each day. I felt optimistic. I was enjoying having less possessions and a simpler daily routine.

As I left our room, I was happier embracing the noise, crowds, and city pollution. I was even enjoying slapping my clothes to get rid of the swarms of annoying flies that collected in the stairwell. I wondered if I was an adrenalin junkie. I was shy as a young child but also super active growing up with four siblings in a busy household. Once I joined my athletics club at fourteen, I began meeting people from all over Melbourne and Australia who expanded my vista to diverse people, and this trip was now helping me do that too. A Shakespearean saying popped into my head: I really wanted *the world to be my oyster*.

Our Last Day in Calcutta

I WOKE UP ready for our last day in Calcutta. I meditated, rolled over, and slept in. My mind was pretty quiet and the morning seemed very still. I wondered if I would ever write any letters home to my family and friends. I wondered if some of my anxious feelings I was picking up from Ryan and Adrian. I felt that this stripped back way of living over the next few months might crystallize directions for what I wanted to do with my life after art school.

We headed off to look around the city and to find a temple to Kali, a Divine Mother goddess of destruction of evil. We looked in at a Rajasthan ivory shop that sold carved boxes and sculptures; some were yellowing while some were colourfully painted. We also checked out the more upmarket shops at the Grand Hotel. Here we met a Buddhist monk who was looking to buy a Buddha image. We started talking and then walking together. He slowed us down with his calm talking, and leisurely pace and mannerisms.

The monk told us a lot about himself and his beliefs. He was from near the border of Burma. He had been a monk for thirty-five years beginning when he was eight years old.

He was a student in Bodh Gaya where Gautama Buddha was enlightened.

He was learning English at the Christian College near the Victoria Memorial Hall. He took us to a teahouse and paid for our black tea with limejuice. The glasses of water there smelt strongly of chlorine. The monk did everything in a calm and steady manner but he was not soft or weak. His personality was strong and extremely charismatic.

We walked in the large open parks nearby. I was looking at a tree that had two sorts of leaves and long brown seeds pods. We went through the gardens up steps to the Victoria Memorial then around and back down. We found a park bench to sit on and I pulled out a book to read while Ryan explained the meanings of English words to the monk. Adrian added in funny Australian definitions to confuse them both. The monk really laughed hard at some of the word puns and wanted to learn the double meanings too.

After a while we said our goodbyes and left him there on the bench. He gave us the contact details of his temple in northern Thailand and asked us to visit and stay. It made us want to go to Bodh Gaya during our travels.

We walked several blocks to the main street where an extremely conservatively dressed man with glasses gave us directions to the temple. We passed many shops and the guys bought small Tamil drums worth about two dollars. They were roughly made but had a light soothing sound. There were also shops with statues, posters, and framed pictures of deities like Ganesh, Buddha, and Krishna.

Then we saw it up ahead. It dominated the surrounding suburban landscape. It was cream coloured but with scalloped multi-coloured trims, elongated with arches and had one tall dome section accompanied by several smaller domes. We had finally found the Kalighat Kali Temple we set out to see this morning. The lanes and shops surrounding it were incredibly dirty and lined with many beggars. There were children calling out to their mothers and a very intense atmosphere in the crowd that mingled at the foot of the high concrete steps into the temple. We learnt that the pools of blood on cutting blocks outside the temple were from goats used as offerings to Kali.

We walked up the steps, ignoring a group of child beggars. A man called out to us to take off our shoes. The children pulled them off our feet, lined them up neatly, and patted them with their hands as if flattening them. We asked some men there to watch our shoes but they assured us that no one wanted to steal them. When we came out, there they were still in a row and no one was even near them.

Inside the temple there were old, dirty flowers, petals, leaves, fruit, big ants, and blood all over the floor. Ryan spoke with a man who said it was a kind of Krishna-Buddhist-Kali temple. I think he was actually trying to give us an overview of all the deities and we got a little confused. It was clearly a Hindu temple. He said that instead of Buddha's statue they had an ornamental red and black statue that may have had the goats' blood on it. I was not really sure if we understood what he was telling us.

It was very serene inside the temple. There were two men either side of the central shrine with metal bowls to collect money but there was no problem if you didn't want to donate. I noticed this same easy attitude in the beggars outside, as they didn't insist on being given money.

There was a man who bought some *prasad*, a religious food, and then squatted to eat it. He then bowed, tapped the wall, rubbed the wall, bowed again, offered petals, and repeated these things as he made his way down a hallway nearby. He went out on to the balcony and bowed to the wall, tapped, rubbed, and rested his forehead on the wall. Watching this man, I realised that devotion could mean anything that you felt inclined to do to express yourself. I enjoyed his sincerity. As we walked outside again, children followed us. We passed their mothers, some goats and cows as we walked to the cable car stop. Visiting the temple was a standout new experience for me.

At home we showered, went out to eat, and ended with a water fight to finish our last meal in Calcutta. It was a great release to throw small glasses of water at each other as we left the restaurant and ran into the street outside. It was so hot that night I slept in my bikini top and lungi skirt. For half the night we left our room door open for cross ventilation.

Calcutta to Kashmir

WEDNESDAY, I WOKE at 4 a.m. I grabbed Ryan's arm to shake him awake as he was so deeply asleep and he woke Adrian. I showered, and then we went down to eat in the dark and quiet breakfast room. We filled our water bottles. While the others showered, I meditated until the hotel manager came to say our taxi had arrived.

We got into our taxi…then we got out of our taxi, as it was the wrong one. We saw our man in a green turban who had quoted us only twenty rupees. We waited for him to drive over.

We arrived at Howrah Junction Railway Station, to board a train as our first step in our three-day journey to Kashmir. Its façade was a huge multistorey red brick building constructed in the 1850s by the East India Trading Company. Inside was a concreted open expanse that led to many simple low roofed platforms. We showed our tickets and entered our platform that was full of people. Many were asleep in rows rolled up in blankets, other around them were cooking in small pots or grooming and preparing for the day, while others were already working. There was a small aisle that we could walk along between those living on the platform and the train. Pollution from the cooking and steam trains filled the space. This scene I will never forget.

We found our seats. There was a huge hockey player sitting opposite me. Hockey had been played in India since the 1920s introduced by the British he said and he played in a top team. He did push-ups off the walls and the luggage rack over our heads. When he went for walks during the journey, I was able to stretch out and wiggle my legs.

There was also a family of a few widows and a couple of quite older men who would not buy food but only eat home prepared food. Everything they used came from a trunk under their seat.

One woman peeled two mangoes and cut off the flesh into a stainless steel mixing bowl. She massaged this plus a heap of sugar and soft rice flakes into a paste with her right hand. She told me the name of the dessert, but I couldn't catch it. Using small pieces of banana leaves as bowls she dished up a generous daub of it for her family and us. It was delicious. We washed our hands with water she poured over her mixing bowl. Then she threw the water out the train window. We also bought vegetarian thalis cooked on the train.

We Arrived in Srinagar

WE ARRIVED IN Srinagar late on Friday night the 25th of May, and stayed at a really ornate houseboat with complex carved trims and furniture, stunning Persian rugs, and silk curtains. It had taken two days and included changing trains, at Haridwar, to get to Jammu, Kashmir. We then took a bus north to Srinagar. It was so quiet and still that night sleeping in a soft bed after constant movement on the hard vinyl or wooden slat beds on the trains.

By Saturday we had moved to another houseboat called the Emperor's Palace where we would stay for one month. This was more reasonably priced and we could use it as a base to explore the town, lakes, and mountains. The altitude was about 5,000 feet above sea level even though Srinagar was in the Kashmir valley area.

The houseboat's owner was Omar, his wife's name sounded like Aliya and their children: a teenage boy Fareed, a ten-year-old daughter Salama, and a baby boy called Nasser. Fareed was about six feet tall and looked thin but strong. He worked a lot with Omar so we would see him daily. He was very friendly and would like to learn English with us. On Sunday we met two cousins, who also worked for Omar.

I explored the boat with interest. It had several bedrooms off a thin hallway. One had an ensuite and there was also a share bathroom. It was a simple wooden construction. It had carved wooden trims and was decorated with many coloured Persian rugs. Its roof was flat and could be covered in rugs, turning it into a lounge where everyone sat or lay down to rest, eat, and drink tea. From here, there were also great views of the surrounding houseboats, lake and mountains.

From the roof I saw the shops along the main road nearby. I would visit them a lot beginning later that first day including: jewellery, embroidery, craft, carpet, and woodwork shops. I bought my parents a hand-woven woollen rug there and posted it home.

I also bought a bottle of saffron honey that first day in the shops. Apparently, there were very few places in the world where bees had access to saffron crops so this was a rare flavour. It was a beautifully aromatic honey, which we ate for breakfast with fresh Kashmiri breads and spiced tea.

Adrian bought two sets of hand cymbals described as being made from an alloy of seven metals.

Both the boys had diarrhoea that day.

The majority of the population of Kashmir was Sunni.

I was reading *How to Know God: The Yoga Aphorisms of Patanjali*. When back in Melbourne I would do more T.M. courses on Patanjali's yoga sutras. Other books I had were commentaries on Vedanta, the Bhagavad Gita, and some of the Upanishads. I wanted to read traditional Indian literature while travelling there.

I also had *The Glass Bead Game* by Herman Hesse.

It was definitely cooler in Srinagar, so Aliya loaned me a heavy, rust-coloured, corduroy phiran to wear over my clothes when cold. It was like a long poncho with a bib front embroidered with silver thread. I thought she might need it back so I decided to get myself some warmer clothes.

Me wearing Aliya's phiran at breakfast on the houseboat roof.

It rained, bringing fresh air that was soothing after the heat of Calcutta. I found the steady patter mesmerising and almost hypnotic as the raindrops made a series of shifting patterns on the lake around the boat. I love watching rain. When young, Mum would sometimes pull back all the curtains and blinds of our large front window, and my siblings and I would line up along the window ledge to watch rainstorms.

On the boat there were other travellers. We were all in our twenties. There was a Swiss woman, two Australian women, and a guy called Peter, in the room next to mine. He wore a jewelled Kashmiri cap.

We also got to know Anna and Tim, an Australian couple from Adelaide, who we'd met on the other houseboat on our first morning in Srinagar. They had been travelling for a year and a half, starting in London, then Morocco and so on back to Australia. We started doing most things with them. I felt very comfortable with them, as they weren't hippies, and weren't looking for drugs like some others.

Ryan and Tim had a paddling class with Fareed so we would all be self-sufficient getting about on shikaras, the gondola-like boats used for transportation on the lake. Ryan and Anna then played chess while Fareed and Tim swam in the lake. Adrian was reading. Tomorrow Anna and Tim were going to try to clear their lungs. Not sure how? Go for a walk? Maybe give up smoking?

As darkness fell, I could hear what sounded like cannon shots, but it turned out that at night tourists liked to set off firecrackers and rockets. Kashmir was peaceful at that time but I felt it didn't hurt to check about things going on around us. Since the 1947 partition of India and Pakistan there had been varying levels of conflict here, with major wars in 1947 and 1966. A ceasefire existed now.

The days on the houseboat were very easy and relaxing. Simple things kept us amused. I liked sitting with Aliya in her tiny kitchen where she turned out all the meals. She worked long hours squatting while peeling, chopping, grinding, and stirring food in metal pots on gas jets. A small door in the wall opened directly on to the lake. She used this to wash all the food, dirty dishes, and pots. She collected lake water to boil for drinking and threw in all the food scraps there too. At home I might be impatient waiting for food to cook. Here I was calm and tolerant. Life was slower.

Dal Lake, Srinagar

I LIKED SHOPPING in Srinagar and posted most of my purchases home. It lightened my pack. Sometimes merchants would also visit our houseboat with antique ivory and bronze pieces.

At a wood carvers' factory I bought three walnut boxes for my sisters and paid with traveller's cheques. There were so many beautifully carved works that it was hard to choose. One box had a tree of life motif on top and the others were covered completely with a decorative leaf pattern. The workers in the factory said they were jewellery or *keepsakes* boxes. They said things change, and we change, but the contents of the box would stay the same.

One day we went to the Dal Lake Swimming Pool. This was much further down the large lake and out in the middle. It was a large houseboat with open spaces and a deck rather than accommodation rooms. Everyone sat in the sun on rugs and deck chairs, or could dive off the boat into the water. They sold drinks and snacks. Ryan and Fareed swam and were happy diving into the lake. I was not a strong swimmer, was not sure how clean the water was and didn't want to strip off, so remained clothed and on board.

Later on I went with Ryan in a shikara to one of the grocery stores in town as he was looking for chess pieces. He was getting the hang of the paddling.

Adrian was losing a lot of weight. We were all worried about his health. I was getting on well with both Ryan and Adrian. It would be sad to see Adrian fly home if he didn't get better soon.

A new person called Sam arrived at the houseboat at lunchtime.

Some days were lazy. Some days I would just go to the shops or do mundane jobs around the houseboat like washing. Sometimes I got restless, as I wanted to see other places.

Another day we visited a papier-mâché factory. This was a large warehouse on the bank of a canal that we reached in a shikara. Stepping up off the boat into the warehouse was like stepping into an older world. There were a variety of piles of cut up newspaper and they showed us the templates and styles of some of their work. There was a vast array of highly decorated and varnished boxes, bowls, plates, and containers. After much deliberation, I bought dinner-sized plates for my older sister and parents.

Two men working there were trying to use English but a lot of it was swearing. They were insulting other factories. Papier-mâché is a popular handicraft in Kashmir and they were disgruntled by all their competition but very happy we had chosen to come to them.

Some days would settle down, wind down, almost to a halt. They were about calmness, isolation and listening to the soundscape, like the cock crowing.

One day we went further into the shopping suburbs. I bought a hand-spun knitted woollen jumper for forty rupees. It was a natural off-white colour, with a high cross-over front collar panel. It reminded me of the woollen jumpers you might see at the Victoria Market in Melbourne. I could wear it at home too. I imagined it had been sitting there waiting for me and wondered for how long. Some of the shops and market stores, and their goods looked ancient to me. We also looked at sets of tabla drums.

Another day Aliya bought a bunch of deep red roses to decorate the houseboat. They filled one very large and two smaller glass vases that I sketched in my diary. The leaves were beautifully round as were the petals. I found myself also picking at and playing with some other potted plants. They had a pretty and delicate, tired, bowed look.

Some days were full of quiet reading, being interested when one of the children brought home stinging nettle, or writing in my diary. I would scribble simple sentences full of incorrect lazy words like: "I walked nimbly but loose armed-lee that quiet needing day." I enjoyed just plucking petals off a fallen rose head. Life had slowed down a lot since Calcutta. If I were at home I would be working and saving to travel. Now while travelling I was doing not much.

Fareed was toying with a fish on a line in the lake one day while I vacantly watched for ages. Later I prepared a parcel to post home. It contained my various purchases including a chillum or wooden pipe requested by my friend Jenny.

I read this today: "to change your mood or mental state—change your vibration. Will directs the attention and attention changes the vibration." Didn't note the book I found it in. Not sure what it meant either. I added quite a few random sentences in my writing, and quotes, or stream of consciousness ramblings.

I was also reading Jean-Paul Sartre's *Intimacy* at the time.

One day we walked about thirteen miles around Dal Lake and a neighbouring lake, including the Rose Garden terraces. The calm, mirror-like surface of the lake reflected the soft blue sky and cumulus clouds above. I felt free and floating in the beauty of this lake and gardens. The pungent smell of the masses and rows of rose bushes were heady and overpowering at times.

We began talking about going to Pahalgam for glacier hiking, starting with a fifty-five mile bus ride. Omar and other people he knew would advise us about what to do and take.

Salama had her friends over for lunch one day, which added lightness to the ambience. Young girls surrounded me while everyone else was out.

I was reading Asimov's story collection *I, Robot*, that I had found in the bookcase on the boat. On page forty-seven: "consider this in comparison to the solar system. ... A ray of light that travels from the Sun to Earth in eight minutes, and to distant Pluto in five and a half hours, could reach even the nearest star after a journey of years." The speed of light was 186,282 miles per second. This gave me a sense of scale and a bigger worldview picture.

After her friends left, Salama came over to me chomping some food in her mouth and pulling faces. She then swung on a wooden pole on the deck. As the pole was on the edge of the boat she flew out over the water as she swung. She was swinging around and around the pole with her back to it, her hands crossed behind her head while holding on. She straightened her back and yelled out towards the distant waters of the lake. She adjusted and recrossed her fingers and continued yelling in Kashmiri as she swung. I had no idea what she was saying, but she was having a great time.

Wearing a loose shirt called a *shalwar,* Salama seemed to have no worries on her mind about fashion. The Kashmiri clothing of a loose pyjama suit seemed so relaxed and easy.

Salama's brown hair was also wildly free, encircling her round face. She had strong, white, wide, separated teeth and big brown eyes. I found some hair elastics that I didn't need due to my recent haircut and gave them to her. With a serious expression, she knotted her hair into a bun for me to see her face and then burst into a broad grin.

She then began pretending she was doing clothes washing, wringing it out while she sang. She brought her little brother over to play with us too. She swung around the pole again and then hugged the baby. We drew together in my sketchbook. I really enjoyed Salama's company as she reminded me of myself at the same age and living mostly in my imagination. I noticed that I had lost most of my travel anxiety. I was resting up, gaining confidence, getting ready to head off again.

That night while we ate, we chatted with Omar's brother-in-law. He had brought over some *tankas*, Buddhist tapestry paintings, to show us. Some of the houseboat guests bought a few from him. He described having gone to trade in Leh in the Indian territory of Ladakh since it opened up in 1974 for tourism. Due to extreme weather it always closed between May and June. When it opened, about 175 trucks per day crossed there taking food into Ladakh and Tibet across the mountains. He said in these regions for centuries the diet had been poor and they ate mostly old potatoes of many varieties, rice, and macaroni.

We were having a run of more sunny days. I would get up early to have a hot shower before breakfast. Perhaps it was getting in first that ensured hot water just like a usual family dynamic. I was enjoying this comfortable feeling but was still restless.

I was reading Jorge Luis Borges short story collection *A Universal History of Infamy*. Reading these fictional accounts of known criminals seemed intense, odd, yet superficial and fanciful while being on holiday on a houseboat in Kashmir exploring very real new people and places. Perhaps the English translation was a little inaccurate too.

I noticed that all the males in Omar's family were confident looking after the baby, Nasser. He never wore nappies either. It seemed they all had a life of physical work but also had a lot of connectedness to each other throughout the day. In contrast, Ryan, Adrian and I were all reading again rather than engaging with one another.

We read anything in the houseboat library. I checked on all the houseboat guests; we had four reading and one sleeping, while three of the houseboat family were working for us around the boat. My family at home was always on the go so there was not much time sitting around reading. I enjoyed this time. I watched the little baby tear small slithers of peeling paint off a wooded beam. A large snow goose flew overhead.

As I read, I was distracted by the floating shopkeepers calling out from their shikaras laden with fruit and vegetables and all manner of things for sale. They made me laugh due to the nonchalance in which they called out bizarre items: Limca, Campa-cola, walnuts, chocolate, cigarettes, apple juice, hashish, mandrax, mescaline, LSD, toilet paper.

Salama and an older woman watched me sketch in my diary and made a game of recognizing which person lying on the roof I was drawing.

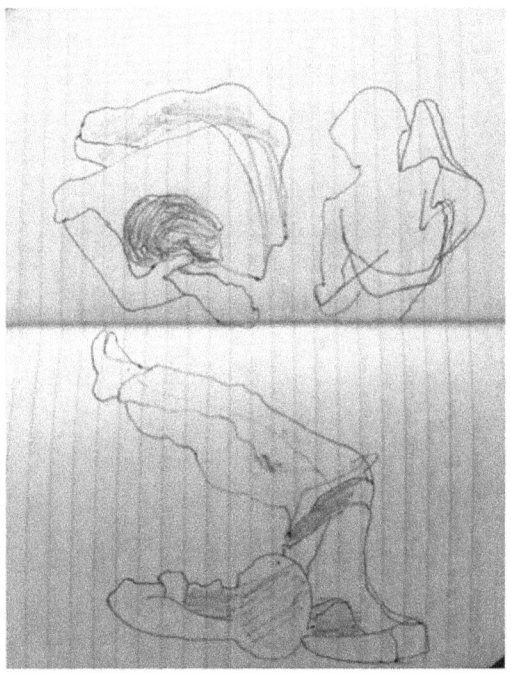

Guys lounging on rugs on the houseboat roof.

Later inside I was reading *The Beginning and the End* by Asimov about the solar system. He described the sun as a "glorious object" in our heavens. Copernicus thought it was the centre of the universe, but it was just merely a star. Further it was merely an ordinary star. There were other stars thousands of times more luminous than our sun but neither was our sun the dimmest. I learnt that the sun was moving towards an apex (relative to closer stars) at a velocity of twelve miles per second. Or was that kilometres? The apex, according to best observations was in a constellation called Lyra, near constellation Hercules.

Aliya was sweeping the lounge and dining room rugs and floor with a homemade broom that was made from a cluster of heavy dry taffeta leaves.

The New Houseboat Hull

THE NEXT DAY was wonderful. It began with a tomato omelette and hot chocolate and ended with a whole roll of photos of our excursion around Srinagar. I didn't usually take many photos as it felt like intruding, but today I took a few. The excursion gave us a lot more interaction with the houseboat people, their working life, and friends.

Our job today was to be part of a large team of friends and family who would help guide the hull of a new houseboat along the Jhelum River. This new houseboat was pivotal for the livelihood of Omar and his family. A new houseboat was another income stream. Steady rent from us and the other tourists had funded this and we were all part of the adventure. The journey took us under various old large bridges and through the old town area of Srinagar. We would end at the boat builder's factory who would build a house on this base. Not many people in the group spoke English but we had the basic idea of what was going on and it was fabulous to be included in this important event.

We took a shikara, and then a taxi with Omar to an agricultural district with crops running along either side of a river that flowed into the Srinagar Lake. He told us it flowed all the way across the top of India to Bangladesh, for their cattle farmers. There were many simple one-room houses along the riverbank made of mud brick, or planks covered with mud. In the distance were snow peaked mountains, hints of valleys, and abundant fluffy clouds.

We all climbed into a very solid, slightly larger shikara. Omar and his nephews paddled us across the very strong current of the wide river. We arrived at a large home that fronted onto the riverbank but was set back behind a large tree.

There were lots of kids running around with chickens and puppies. Roosters kept crowing. The riverbank and surrounding land was compacted and shiny mud, like the floor inside the mud brick houses. Everyone had bare feet except the Australian contingent so perhaps the bare feet polished the mud.

We crossed over into the next yard and walked along thick wooden planks onto the hull of the new houseboat. The children were all screaming a lot while one mother sat calmly feeding a happy cherub-faced baby.

We then had four hours sitting around waiting for a powerboat. There were other things that had to be done in the meantime. We learnt that one of the nearby sheep had to be slaughtered before we could leave. The meat would then be given to the poor who lived around here. A butcher came and slit its throat, hung it up in a tree at the river's edge, and let the blood drain into the water.

After that the sheep carcass was thrown on the riverbank. It looked a little blown up like a balloon. Without its head now it was hung again and fleeced. It seemed as if the fleece just peeled off. The meat was then cut up into baskets. Then it was further divided into small pieces. One big piece was put into the fleece and thrown onto the hull of the houseboat. There was no refrigeration.

It had been quite hot and sunny but now the sun receded behind the clouds. As my friends and I were vegetarians we ate salad sandwiches and drank Persian tea served from a large copper teapot that tasted of cinnamon, cardamom, and lemon. Omar and all the men ate a mutton, potato, and rice meal with bread rolls. I had only been a vegetarian for two or three years and had grown up eating large meat portions. I was amazed at the small sized servings of meat they all ate.

Next Omar gave the builders of the hull and everyone a few instructions about how we would all work together to move it down the river. Then a powerboat arrived. He described it as having a six-stroke, foot cranked, hand air filtered, clogged fuel etcetera engine. I wasn't that interested in the details but loved travelling along the river. Driving the powerboat was a young Norwegian guy in white shorts. Omar and the other men included Ryan and Tim in conversations. I really just was enjoying the day out in nature with a large group of people. For most of them it was work. Without much responsibility it felt like a party for me.

It took a few hours for the hull to be pulled by the powerboat many miles along the river. At times several men on the riverbank also helped pull it using long thick ropes. Many others including Ryan and Tim used their hands and wooden poles to keep the hull from crashing into walls, homes, or other obstacles along the banks. At times the river narrowed a lot.

Some of the people on the hull, such as, the children and I, were really there as spectators. We were appreciated as audience for our *oohs* and *aahs*, and our praise of them when tricky situations were overcome. It was a really enjoyable day.

The river water was part of their lives in so many ways. It flowed through the old and historic part of Srinagar. We passed many temples, mosques, and houses, some with grass roofs. We saw the Raja's Palace, behind, which were the stunning, snow-covered mountains. We carefully manoeuvred under many old, yet strong and heavily populated wooden bridges where the strong current of the river would swing us sideways. Some bridges had long rolls of recently block printed or washed fabric hanging from them while they dried. They said this area was where the fabric printing factories were.

There were many people watching from the bridges and town as we passed. There was constant saluting and calling out of "Salam" between the people on the hull and the people on the riverbanks. Our people paid respects to shrines as we passed. There were donations put on the poles and handed to the poor. I felt part of their community for the day.

At one point the speedboat that was pulling us conked out and stopped dead. It had a fuel blockage and had overheated. While we waited for it to spring back to life, we saw we had stopped near a large mulberry bush. Omar shook the bush and directed the berries to fall down into the hull. We picked them up and shared them around. We gave three big branches full of fruit to Aliya to take home for later. This reminded me of picking blackberries in bushy areas near home before Glen Waverley was developed.

At one point we also towed a middle-aged tourist couple in their shikara. As the current was strong in parts of the river, we lost them under one bridge, but picked them up again a while after that. A man in another shikara was trying to sell us all cushions by following us along.

It started to rain lightly, so I moved from my position on the very front of the hull behind its rim. I went back into the middle main floor that was lower and slightly protected from the wind. There, Aliya had been making *billy* tea over a gas jet; everything all stewed up in one pot—tea, milk and sugar. I savoured my cup, which was delicious with bread rolls. I then took a few pictures of our group on the hull.

As we entered Dal Lake there was even less space to get through and there was a lot of yelling as the waterways were clogged up with many shikaras. We came dangerously close to a kindergarten and college so men climbed on nearby doongas (larger canoes with a roofed middle section) to help push the hull too.

If the houseboat hull was damaged or damage was done to the buildings on the riverbank then today would be a disaster. Either situation might cause financial ruin. Everyone strained to work towards a safe journey home.

I was watching the two carpenters that managed the hull move and worked steadily all day with Omar, their client. They were brothers who looked almost identical and were very good looking.

I sat with Aliya mostly and she gave me some small red roses to smell and butterscotch lollies to eat, while we watched everyone work. We didn't speak much but I had become accustomed to hanging out with her and we were relaxed and happy together. As we observed everything that passed us by on the riverbanks, our heads swivelled back and forth like spectators at a tennis match.

We saw a guy we knew standing on the patio of a hotel along the river with two large Indians. His name was Tony and had been staying on our houseboat earlier on. We saw streets full of shops and shoppers, traffic, many doongas, and shikaras with sellers calling out. Turning one corner, our hull squashed an empty shikara moored by a rope to the riverbank. It made creaking noises as we pushed off it.

On one bank we picked up a white shirted *uncle* who brought on board a leg of lamb and a large bag of rice for us to take home.

We went into a canal lock, waiting for the water level to rise, the men ran off onto the banks behind buildings or trees for a wee and Aliya hopped off to shop.

Omar and I were left behind. He had noticed me spending the day with his wife. He wanted to talk about her while she was absent. He told me when he was twenty-five his father had chosen Aliya to be his wife. She was twenty. He was happy with her but had originally wanted a *westerner* but at least now with the houseboat business he was able to meet many people from other countries, which he liked.

When everyone returned we went through the lock with everyone pushing off one of its walls and then dropped off a few people on the steps near the next bridge. They caught hold of a parked shikara to use as a step to get off the hull.

We spoke with a man selling cauliflowers and gave him a tow.

We passed a girls' school where students in white hijabs with blue dresses lined up along the windows. We were entertaining them. Outside more students pressed up along the hurricane fence, making it sway.

Later our small houseboat group jumped off the hull onto the embankment. Ryan and Tim helped me off, as it was a really wide jump. We waved goodbye to Omar and Aliya and their family and friends.

We went up the bank to the road, walked and then ran to a bus stop. Luckily I got a seat near the window on the bus so I could continue taking in the sights of the old town of Srinigar. So much history in this city settled about 2,000 years ago. We rode past shops and restaurants, and a beautiful fort but the stunning Nanga Parbat range of snowy mountains held my gaze.

We hopped off the bus at our usual markets. On the corner was a cake and lolly shop where I got my favourite walnut slice.

Old town Srinigar riverbanks.

Old town Srinigar, new block printed fabric drying on a bridge.

Old town Srinigar riverbanks.

Moving the new hull along the river through old town Srinigar.

Moving the new hull.

Afternoon tea break on the new hull.

We walked excitedly along the road to our shikara pick-up spot. Ryan helped Fareed over a wall. Fareed was tired from working all day but rowed us slowly to the houseboat. There were lots of jokes with Anna and Tim who were rocking the boat to keep him awake. A small amount and then a large amount of water came into the boat. As we were getting out Tim was joking around again with Fareed and instead of helping him out he first dipped his rear end down a little towards the water. He was trying to make out his rowing was the trouble. We all thought it was funny. Tim was in a good mood and it was infectious.

We told Adrian all about the great day we had and enjoyed his quick-witted responses. He mostly stayed home these days because he was weak and unwell. This meant that Ryan and I had plenty of time together and became closer yet were still reticent to begin a relationship.

I was completely overstimulated. I was high on laughing, as I often was with friends back home. It felt good to laugh. I was sick of being quiet and reading. I needed more adventures. Some kind of energy was building up. I hadn't been running in a while. I couldn't calm down to meditate so did some yoga instead, read about Sri Lanka in a book I'd found, then finally did meditate.

More Time on the Houseboat

I WAS ENJOYING having my own room at the moment. The boys were doing a long and difficult session of yoga on the roof and I did a little yoga plus meditation as usual. I had been reading about Ayurveda and found that in that system it was best to lie down on your left side after food and for good sleep you lie on your right side. We were all trying to help Adrian with his stomach.

Ryan and I were talking a lot about getting ready for trekking, so we went into town to buy a few supplies. We also looked at tablas.

I had settled into a series of regular food treats at some of the local shops including slices, cakes, or smoothies. At home I was addicted to saving, except for essentials and spent very little. So this was a new habit.

Later while we were sitting on the riverbank with Adrian, Ryan asked us if we cared about anything, as we must care about something. Adrian said that it was not that he cared about nothing but that he cared about everything and he didn't know where to begin.

After a while I answered that I thought this meant that Adrian did care about many things. In those days I was quite quiet at times and had not found a confident voice yet to speak freely about personal things. I felt deeply about things but often didn't voice those thoughts. I didn't want to contradict anyone and was still figuring out what I really thought. I was taking my time and trying to think for myself, whatever that meant.

Later I said that I cared about the wide winged eagles that glide over my head every day here. There was one preening itself yesterday as it sat on the canal lock gates when we were there.

I tried to think things through, Adrian talked them through, and Ryan was more passionate, almost fighting to work things out that way.

On our shikara ride home we found out the boy from a neighbouring houseboat was an English teacher. A young girl and her chaperone were going to his doonga for a lesson, which he moved around the lake like a mobile school.

That night Adrian bought two more temple finger bells and Ryan bought a tanka of Nataraja, the Hindu god of dance, a form of Shiva. Ryan had taken up dancing before we had left Australia and wanted to do more.

That night I slept on the roof along with Aliya who was very tired from the day out. I was kept awake by the moonlight as the moon moved across the sky over a few hours. The moon eventually went down and I slept. It had been really cooling sleeping on the houseboat roof before the sun came up but then it began to get quite hot.

At dawn there were many large dragonflies that sounded and looked like helicopters. A neighbour who saw us up on the roof brought over her nine-month-old baby who Aliya loved kissing and playing with. Stunning eagles were gliding above again too.

After breakfast we were downstairs again sitting on the outer steps, while Adrian and Ryan were discussing working independently of art institutions. They would rather do projects without having to prove anything. They thought this would be a more peaceful way to work. They felt they needed a quiet and passive state of mind to maximize their energy, inflow and outflow of ideas unencumbered by galleries, universities, government grants and bodies.

In my mind I thought it shouldn't matter but maybe they were right. I needed to just keep making art. I wanted to make some good work and exhibit. I was interested in all media but in non-representation. I was working towards less and less representation towards simple colour fields in my paintings. My brother always teased me, saying, "Can you do another landscape?" as I had done at high school.

An old man with a bristle-covered face stirred us out of our middle class conversation. He was rowing over to our houseboat with his right hand and holding two yellow flowers in his left hand. He came up close to Ryan and me, mumbling slowly. He asked Ryan if he wanted to buy the wilted flowers for his girlfriend. I shook my head. I indicated with my pen that I was writing and said no, nodded goodbye, and he eventually mumbled at us and then left. Ryan was impressed that the man could row with only one hand. Perhaps he should have paid for a rowing lesson from him instead.

This morning Ryan spoke a lot about what he would like to do when he went back to Melbourne. He wanted to have a house with Mark, another artist friend, with two studios, one for each of them. He wanted to work with a drama group at their yoga centre. He rarely spoke about his art making. I was often sketching and taking photos. Ryan spoke about all his friends and how some wanted to go to the country to live and some just wanted to exhibit artwork in Melbourne. He seemed a bit lost to me, but then weren't we all looking for something with this trip?

I was listening and watching life going by on the lake. A young girl who I had noticed a lot lately was rowing her shikara furiously and speeding along. There was someone trying to soothe a screaming baby with funny little noises. There was a man riding a bicycle along the road across the lake and whistling the tune "A Bicycle Built for Two." His whistling gradually morphed. He changed to classical music and was accompanied by the sound of a nearby duck flapping its wings while washing. Another backing vocal was the guttural noise of someone clearing their throat and then the sound of teeth being brushed. One of our European neighbours added a steady, soft splashing sound as another layer of percussion as he swam in the lake.

I could see marijuana plants growing freely along the edges of the lake.

I had now turned my mind back to Melbourne and my art practice too. I was wondering if I would continue making art when I went back. I recalled things people had said about my work and that I must continue. I had developed a respiratory reaction to working with solvents with my printmaking and painting so I was questioning which medium I could use. It has taken me two or three years to sort out my approach and order of techniques in my prints, and now I had to just walk away and leave them due to asthma.

That night I played card games with Salama. I also went out with Ryan on a shikara but we got stuck on a tree stump. After we freed the boat I had dinner in town with Ryan but Adrian stayed back as he was not well again.

When back on the houseboat Salama kept saying, "She mean to me" as a joke when I was drawing instead of playing with her.

Fareed said he had been making a very colourful painting of a houseboat in the moonlight for months but lost it. He also had a small bottle of brandy. He wanted to have a drink tonight but I wasn't interested.

We all slept under the stars on the roof that night, under a hazy moonlit sky. One side of the moon was soft so it would be fuller tomorrow night. I was woken up with the heat of the sun as it was rising. The early morning mist on the lake created a soft, wide sheet of brilliant light that spread across the mountains, hiding the horizon line. It was so sublime and reminded me of colour field paintings. I felt nostalgic for art making and felt a pinch that I couldn't share these beautiful places and moments with my friends and family. My Dad would have liked to travel more. Mum preferred being at home.

I tried doing a sketch of the scene but it was impossible. My line drawing would not work to adequately capture this beautiful vision.

Salama was still saying, "She mean" when I walked around the roof and headed downstairs. We made messy cooking together again today.

Adrian had decided to go to London. He had continued to lose weight and was not getting any better. He needed medical input and time to get stronger again. He was not enjoying India much at all. He had an uncle in London so would go and stay with him. I would miss him and his wit. Our mood was subdued. Ryan and I couldn't really agree on the next stages of our travel. It seemed inevitable that we would all split up. We went to the city centre of Srinagar with Adrian as he organised flights. I got stung on my middle left toe by a wasp. So now I was limping. We went out to dinner and planned to go for a walk afterwards in the cool of the evening but we overate and went home instead to lie down on the houseboat.

Ryan talked a lot about himself, where might we travel and when. Shall we go for a trek? Will I come with him? I told him I'd see what happens; I might stay just a bit longer. I might go for the trek. I might look for art galleries on the way back into India. What were my reasons for travelling? For me it's a need to experience a change or a break. For Ryan it was about anti-materialism. He commented that now he knows he's more Marxist than he thought. After Calcutta he felt India was becoming *westernised* so he was not so interested in more travel there.

I still wanted to travel with Ryan but I didn't want to stay in Kashmir the whole trip. I started thinking about things that I would actually like to do rather than just following along. I had heard about some Abstract Expressionist art, contemporary German arts, and Post-expressionist art in some Kashmir galleries. I wanted to go seek them out. I was so full of food, it was hard to think and plan.

I was reading *The Agony and the Ecstasy*.

I was sunbaking today on the houseboat roof and wrote letters to several friends back home.

Adrian called his Mum to tell her he's going to London to stay with his uncle there.

Fareed did not want to go to school when he was young but now wished he had. Tim supported him saying maybe it was a shame he didn't go to school.

I'm reading a lot today and learning about different types of stars from Eddington's *Stellar Evolution Theory* from the 1920s.

I wrote pages of it down in my diary to try to understand it, but then found out that this theory only lasted a decade though his career was well respected. Ha.

Adrian Went to London While We Went to Yusmarg

TODAY ADRIAN WAS going to London and we were going up into the mountains. I hoped he'd be okay travelling on his own. He was glad to be leaving. It was a quick parting of ways. It felt too quick for me and I would have preferred to take him to the airport to make sure he was all right.

Our trip changed today and I knew I would head off in my own direction soon. Ryan and I caught a bus to a town called Charar-i-Sharief in the countryside. I enjoyed sitting on the bus with a woman with her two young daughters. At the end of the line we got off and walked, as past this point there were no buses.

We walked for about five minutes before a truck pulled over to give us a lift. It had multicoloured decoration at the front and the sides. We threw our bags up and into the back of the truck and climbed in. The driver took us two miles up the hill. We then walked again and found a taxi to Yusmarg, a serene green hill station with a backdrop of the stunning snow-covered mountains of the Pakistan border. It was less than one hundred miles as the crow flies to Islamabad.

We stayed in a hotel on the hill. It was free for us as the proprietors were friends with our houseboat family. Dinner cost only 8 rupees. I was given a bed while Ryan was called *the boy* and told to sleep on the floor in the living area.

We had a cold-water wash out of a big orange bucket in the morning. We walked along a very rocky riverbed. We hired ponies and rode to Dilda Gunga, where there were beautiful brown rocks on the river. Walking across soft green hills on our way back to the hotel, we met the Indian weightlifting team. They all wore army uniforms but were training for the Olympics and were huge muscle-bound guys.

Ryan was in a chatty mood and was telling me lots of stories about his friends, about school, and past girlfriends that I had not heard before. He also said my main art school lecturer had told him to "Look after her", meaning me. I took offense as I could run faster than Ryan. What was he thinking? What were they both thinking? Sometimes I did feel as if Ryan spoke down to me. I guess he was confiding in me more because Adrian had left. He often seemed to be trying to work out his relationship with women. Was he trying to work me out too? I listened but didn't have much to say.

We began making our way back to Srinagar from Yusmarg, by walking seven miles to Nilnag, a stunning lake area. I was used to walking at home and catching public transport often on my own to go to athletics meets. I enjoyed these walks and exercise in general as I felt alive and loved the incredibly fresh air here. There were green rolling hills, forest, and countryside.

The rain had blocked roads and some university students were demonstrating so there were no buses or taxis running. We found ponies and rode with their owner who would then bring them back from Nilnag. Next we got on a really new bus about 4:30 p.m. We passed areas filled with workers in rice paddies, crops of beans, and green vegetables. There were many other workers carrying large pots, baskets of vegetables, and piles of tiffins (meal containers).

Back on the Houseboat

RETURNING TO THE houseboat felt like coming home. I had become comfortable here without the intensity of responsibility, at our escapist pretend home, but I couldn't stay forever.

I shook Omar's hand, the father of the house, and had a cup of tea with Aliya, the mother. We then all sat and ate dinner together. It was too polite for a real family. I was used to more jokes and silliness with mine. After dinner everyone was fixing a doonga to put where an older and now removed Snow Goose Houseboat had been, next to our houseboat.

We were part of the domestic scene here now. Fareed was drawing pictures again. This one was of a girl floating in the sky while holding the strings of puppets below her on the ground and her mouth was blowing a kiss. It looked like a Chagall drawing. Omar handed me a letter from a friend from Melbourne. That night I was happy but cried a bit as I went to sleep from exhaustion as we had been walking so much.

Life had a steady pace now. With Adrian gone our days passed lazily. I had a few bruises on my legs from getting on and off boats and some gravel rash on my bottom from sleeping on the rooftop. My skin healed surprisingly quickly here. I got up early, I meditated, I wrote, and I read. Sometimes I sat and watched lotus flowers open on the lake water. Ryan saw a mouse in the toilet today.

For breakfast one day we had chips, bread and butter, and the non-vegetarians shared a carp that someone had caught in the lake. It was lying on the porch gulping and flapping for air.

Today I was writing back to Mum and some friends whose letters I had just received. When I went to post my letters I collected four more: another from Mum and three from other old friends. I really enjoyed hearing what was going on at home. Some of them were also travelling. They all seemed happy but there was a sense that I was a bit odd, not only going to art school, but now off overseas to unusual places.

Later Salama kidnapped me along with baby Nasser. She took us on a shikara to visit Omar's sister and family.

One of the girls working there was nineteen years old and was telling me about marriage. She brought me a cup of tea and the sugar pot on a tin tray. She also talked about many random things as she was practising English. For example, she said, "On your houseboat you have birds nesting in a triangular window on the east side of the house" and that she had a window like that too. She also said, "The sun every morning comes in and various noises wake me up; there was the tweeting of birds, the gurgling of the tap water, or workers' noises like drilling and cutting".

That night we stayed up later than usual. Some of the men were drinking a pink coloured milky hash tea. Ryan came later to this houseboat and was again discussing many schemes like travelling home perhaps via Spain.

The next morning I took some breakfast into Ryan's room to give him breakfast-in-bed. We talked more and more about our possible futures. We shopped from passing shikara shops. We helped with the repairing of a doonga boat. I contributed by recycling big nails by hammering them flat again. I sat on the front of another doonga nearby while I was working.

I was sewing up a couple of tears in my clothes and thinking about how Adrian might be getting along in London. I was also thinking about friends back home and today I did really miss them. I tried to do several different sorts of work each day: writing, drawing, painting, sewing, reading, and decision-making. I'm trying to convince myself to just go with the tide.

I did a nice long set of yoga asanas, pranayama, and meditation. I balanced these lazy days with physically active days of walking all around Srinagar.

Salama, my "She mean" young friend, had a haircut and then we went out to buy milk for everyone's tea; we all drank a lot of tea. Tim said he liked real milk with "floaters" in it, which sounded so Aussie to me. Some days the cows ran dry and there wasn't enough for the town.

I was excited because tomorrow I was going to the library to get more books. How sad was that? I was starting to get a bit bored here. I would go somewhere else soon after the trek, as I was not ready to go home. I still had money and time left. It would also be a good day for Ryan as he picked up his carved walnut wood chess pieces, which he ordered when we visited the factory ages ago. The library was closed so instead I exchanged my walking boots from size nine to size five.

Omar was teaching Ryan about what he believed and said thongs, clothes, and other material things were not truly yours or mine. We're just lucky to have things while we do.

I was reading Teilhard de Chardin's *The Future of Man*.

Over the next few days I talked with Anna and Tim about travelling with them soon back down into India via Rishikesh. Before leaving Kashmir we all agreed that we wanted to do the shikara trek and also the trek to the Kolahoi Glacier that Omar was planning for us.

I just finished reading Plato's *The Last Days of Socrates*.

Shikara Trek

ON SUNDAY WE headed off into the lake on our shikara trek with the doonga repaired and made comfortable for this four-day outing that cost us each 350 rupees.

I was the only single girl in the group. Along with Ryan there was Anna and Tim, Omar and two men working for him. I was to sleep on the boat at night moored and tied up on the canal banks while everyone else would sleep on the riverbanks nearby. We visited papier-mâché and rug-weaving factories. At times the men pulled the boat along and one cooked for us on the banks of the canals. We had simple rice and dhal meals with boiled vegetables like beetroots. We were travelling through a stunningly beautiful valley filled with lush farmland, forests, and lakes, with mountains all around us. There was often an eagle in the air on these waterways.

I woke the first morning of the trek to a thick fog. It was so deeply silent and I was alone and floating in a dense, soft space that was mildly damp. As the sun came out and the fog cleared I could see goatherds in the trees nearby. The surface of the canal was covered with thick floating deep green moss that looked like clusters of peas. The sunrise produced smoky yellows, oranges and pinks that lazily shone shards of brilliant light through the fog bringing warmth.

Using a long pole, ropes, and at times paddles, our guides moved the boats along. The men and boys washed and swam in the canals. Tim fell in the water once trying to grab the rod. We moved along steadily to Shadipur, a small fishing town.

We ate at the local docks and drank sheep's milk. My hands were becoming very brown on the top like Salama's. Sometimes we played cards, like gin rummy.

The second night I slept out in the open on the riverbanks in a tent with Ryan. It felt too wobbly to sleep in the shikara. Anna and Tim were in a tent but that was okay as they were married. Since Ryan and I were not married, Omar wanted me sleeping separately but he conceded mostly when I said Ryan and I were like brother and sister.

The myna birds chirped and flapped madly if you walked near them.

I had an irrational repetitive feeling that I didn't want to stay too much longer in Kashmir. I craved more travelling and freedom.

Meditating in the tent I kept opening my eyes as I felt the need to watch the world outside. Ryan and I were laughing a lot with Tim as we rolled up the tent. I had a swim in Ryan's shorts then Tim had a swim in Ryan's shorts.

These were long days so I always ate a large breakfast of eggs and bread. I had to dress behind trees. I was reading *The Agony and the Ecstasy* again.

Today I had no time sense. I didn't know where I was and who I was.

I worked out a message that Omar signalled at a distance, to watch the reeds in the water moving slowly, which was like ballet.

Existentialism, the nature of the will of each individual person as a free agent responsible for her own development became very clear to me during the shikara trek. I should go south without Ryan to follow the pull I was sensing. I did not want to stay here for a whole year. We had been here nearly one month already. I could meet Ryan later in New Delhi and we could go to Rishikesh together. We were both interested in yoga and meditation and Rishikesh was all about that. It would be sad to leave Ryan, which is why I mulled it over so much. I didn't know why he wanted to stay. It made no sense. I wanted to see more places and he did not anymore.

I found myself looking at the beautiful shiny round cooking pots. I helped cook dinner as the boys were still working on the doongas on the riverbanks.

I woke up the next morning and looked around in the very moist park, where we had camped alongside the canal and saw an optical illusion. It appeared that two white park benches were floating in the distance in the fog.

Later we visited an art camp set up on another canal bank. We met a guy called Javide, a lecturer in art from Madras University, who was camping with ten other artists. Each day they painted a picture. They paid for the camp by selling these pictures, which then paid for their supplies of paint, studio space, and printmaking materials.

The artists drew each other to see what was the same and what was different. They were looking for specific visual character traits. They talked about their goal that *education is learning about yourself and the universe*. They were looking for balance and moderation in all things and asked each other what they did too much, or too little, in order to change. We all agreed that it was a wonder we can even all talk to each other due to different viewpoints.

Ryan and I always liked opposite things. I tried consciously to harmonise different opinions. I noticed I was almost asking permission or forgiveness as I followed-up previous conversations. That was becoming tiresome, so I would try to let that go.

We looked through some of the paintings from the artists at the camp. I asked them about their work. I discussed the abstract elements in the works in the red reflection of the sun and the grey reflection of snowy mountain peaks.

I asked the students about the possibility of me working in India at an art school although it was highly unlikely I would stay.

Javide spoke about what he was working on at the moment too; lino cuts, watercolours, and teaching English literature at a college in Srinagar.

We also saw a school teaching carving in a park on the canal banks and teenage boys bathing, throwing stones, and screaming in the canals.

We then travelled into wider canals where we could glide more quickly and later tied up our boat on the bank of a big lake for lunch.

In the afternoon we sat under a Chinar tree drinking tea and then ran further down the river bank to a Hindu shrine.

Afterwards we collected green walnut cases. I was also collecting lumps of soil and stones to use as pigments and then relaxed again, sitting in the sun with my back to the side of a mountain.

The sky was a soft blue, graduating to white.

Shikara trek.

I was watching an old Muslim man praying. Then I watched him wrap long white fabric into a turban-like-hat around his head while he began walking up towards the Hari Parbat hill and its Maghul fort that overlooked Srinagar. That hill area also had Hindu and Sikh temples and shrines.

I was remembering my friends and imagining trying to explain why I was staying away for so long. In the past I felt I had done what was expected of me. Now I was trying to find some balance. Some part of me felt selfish as I flew out of Melbourne leaving everyone behind with responsibilities. A gap year was a huge luxury. I had worked for it and it felt like it was a time for me, before I knuckled down to commitments.

I watched some young good-looking athletic Sikhs playing with a super healthy dog. This pet was bouncing around happily. Another dog, a bitch with many sagging teats, was also there moving slowly and looked very tired. A man in a very rough fabric coat called her.

The Kashmiri women usually married young. I saw them often laughing very hard, loudly and freely. They had strong yet pretty features and looked very hard working.

Then we were back in the boats and moving along again. That night we camped in a park at the far end of Dal Lake near a mosque. We went to a very clean market and saw many shops selling gold jewellery. I bought a packet of cornflakes and some Kashmiri flatbread and tea.

I woke up thinking it was morning but it was still dark so I did five minutes of meditation and went back to sleep again. Then Ryan woke up, got out and opened the tent flap, inviting in the searing sun. We both slept again. Later I got out and went to some dirty public toilets. I came back and put some food together for an initial breakfast. We would have more to eat later when home. We would have a relatively shorter journey back to the houseboat today.

I was feeling very even. We found a beautiful smooth lush lawn near our campsite so we took off our shoes and began walking on it until a man called out, "Get off the lawn!"

I enjoyed easy and relaxed times with Ryan on this trek and sharing a tent. The dynamics had changed, as I was his only buddy on this trip now.

There was a haze that made the sunlight like a bright sheet of white; it was blinding. Ryan was sitting in that brightness at the front of the doonga as we were going to another mosque, market, milk cart, and a wood shop for supplies.

To enter the mosque we had to cover our heads with a white shirt or anything else. The walls were made from marble blocks and there was a massive circular pattern inside the domed ceiling. On the floor there were rows of large mats, and four ivory marble steps leading up to a carved walnut wood pulpit high on one wall. As we walked up to the door I was asked, "Are you a girl?" Nearby there was a little boy and three little girls hitting washing. We were asked for a donation for the shrine fund.

We went back on the boat and continued. We saw what looked to be a thick lentil soup moss on the water and reeds in the lake. We turned towards a Hindu temple to the right and then to the Emperor's Palace, our houseboat.

New Travellers

TONIGHT WE MET some new travellers who had come to stay. "Hey!" boomed out at us in an Aussie accent as we arrived there. This was from Tony, who collected specimens for natural history museums, and his partner Dutch Kate. The other couple was Helen and Jordan. Helen worked as a psychologist and sociology teacher at Monash University in Melbourne. Jordan was a farm and pub worker from Bendigo. I was really happy to see some new faces but it meant that Ryan and I had to sleep on the roof again until their rooms became free. We got a much-reduced rate for this, as we also had to use the communal bathroom.

I helped cook the dinner of green beans, potatoes, rice, and curry with paneer cheese. The cubed pieces were fried, then cooked into the vegetables with caraway seeds and eaten with chapattis.

In the morning two Americans arrived too. This last new couple, Adam and Dafna, liked to join in the cooking as well. They made flour balls, rolled them up and cooked them as little pancakes.

Fareed was teaching English words to Aliya, his mother. I played with Nasser, the baby. Hadar had also started working hard on his English.

Salama had now begun school and over the next few days we noticed that she was avoiding us, as she was not happy. She was being bullied. Schoolboys were beating her and throwing stones at her. Many didn't want girls to go to school here. I had a safe education environment and had gone to an all girls' school so this was way out of my comfort zone. I felt really anxious for her.

We were out on a shikara all talking about this, paddling against the tide in a rank smelling canal. Ryan and I were talking about how violence breeds violence. A doonga floated past with Dylan playing.

We all went to a cake shop. Ryan was handing around some dates and then flipped over to talking about why he and I were not a couple, or not even dating. People often asked if we were a couple, especially since Adrian left. I simply thought the answer was that we were *just friends*, end of story. Ryan had clearly been thinking about it a bit more. He often said lightly that we were good but *not that good*. He was really trying too hard, labouring the point, to make it clear that we were just friends and not a couple. I did not think of him romantically as he was way too intense for me.

I paddled back with one of the guys steering. Tim and I made lassi for everyone with lemons, sugar, and water. A dog was wandering up and down on our houseboat.

Aliya said it was too hot for cooking with fire on these long hot days. Due to her culture she wore two long-sleeved tops and a veil. She thought it was okay for the others and me to roll up our trousers and wear a bikini top. She said she would like to live in Australia where she could wear fewer clothes.

We had a communal night with all the guests sitting around playing cards and discussing our next travel ventures. Will we go to Gulmarg? Will we check out the art school in Srinagar? Will we go to the tourist office for options?

I doubted myself in what I'd do next. I had more doubt than I thought. Somehow, others' opinions were still important. I was tired. I wanted to go to Rishikesh soon, but I wanted to wait for some letters that I knew were coming.

I was reading about Patanjali's Yoga Sutras again, the early days of Transcendental Meditation, Gurdjieff and all sorts of philosophies. We talked about The Kybalion, a study of the Hermetic philosophy of Ancient Egypt and Greece. I practised one type of meditation but was open to studying diverse philosophies. I thought I was overtired. I was thinking too much.

Directedness of the individual and our development was the strong topic of conversation and everyone was looking for clarity. There were so many people in the houseboat. We couldn't go to bed, as the lounge was our rooftop bedroom too. Someone criticised my meditation. After playing cards I was beyond tired, as we couldn't go to sleep until after everyone left the roof. I felt like crying. I was not expressing my negative emotions to other people. I was clearly being too polite. I felt restless and really wanted to travel more. I was also missing my good friends back home.

I had breakfast with Ryan, Aliya, and her mother was also there. We talked about so many things. Salt was good for your teeth. Do you know about *Nunchi*, the Korean concept for listening and gauging other people's moods? More people came and were planning today to have haircuts, then to tour a papier-mâché factory and a painting factory.

Ryan wanted to go to India in September and I wanted to go now in June. We agreed to disagree and I didn't really try to persuade him to come as he was set in his ideas. I thought I might like to go off on my own anyhow but I would miss him. It might be harder but I would work that out. I was trying to be brave.

That night we slept on the roof again as it was cool but I had to run to the toilet twice. I had a hot shower in Anna and Tim's bathroom in the morning.

We took the doonga and let Jordan, Helen, Ryan, and Omar off at the bridge near town. Tim and Fareed paddled on to a card game and to knife shops.

I was sunbaking on the roof until Fareed, the wind, and other local clowns came along. I worked with Fareed on his English but he lost patience. He said, "I do want to learn but it's a pity I didn't go to school". He said with his father's encouragement he left school at age ten and also that the boys were caned for nothing.

I had six letters to read from Mum, sisters, and my friends. One was leaving for London soon.

Again we had a good communal night on the houseboat. We all talked about trekking and spiritualism. Dafna and Adam told us about being Jewish Americans.

There were eight for dinner. It was a big meal with a few dishes: rice, chapattis, tomato and mutton, eggplant and potatoes, cabbage and potatoes, and red kidney beans. We played cards until late and some of us slept in the lounge room.

Fareed formally asked me to teach him English. He knew how to write the alphabet and their sounds. We did phonetic spelling, added some rules, and gave examples of those that differ from the norm. I corrected it when he wrote.

We went to the stonecutters' factory with Omar and he ordered a steel wire saw to use for maintenance around the houseboat. It would arrive in twelve weeks. We went to a carpet factory where Dafna and Adam made a deposit on a large red geometric rug. They thought we all should be more polite with Omar, as we had been very forward and invited ourselves to go with him to a big wedding on Sunday.

We took a bus and walked for the 2 p.m. session of lunch at the Hazratbal Mosque. We sat outside on the grass. This was one of the parks where we had camped on the canal trek. I sat in lotus, which was so comfortable on the grass after weeks of yoga on wooden floors. Omar talked to us about the Muslim religion, the up-coming wedding, and how all religions were the same.

We then went to Omar's brother's house for tea and bread, as the buses were too full to get home. Later on we caught a bus to Dal Gate and caught a shikara home. I hung out with Kate and Tony. I had a good long friendly chat with them that afternoon. They were living in another boat now and said that I could come and meditate there any time and perhaps go to the temple with them tomorrow.

I also visited and had a cup of tea with Dafna and Adam at their flashy new houseboat. On the way back I saw a wall mural of a gunman shooting.

Planning a Trek, Drawing, a Mosque Visit, and a Wedding

ONE NIGHT OMAR called me in to a meeting to organise the glacier trek with Tim, Anna, Adam, Dafna, Ryan, and myself. We talked about it and played cards until after 2 a.m. Again we slept on the roof, and with Fareed also. He was scrunched up into a ball of blankets at dawn.

The next day Ryan, Dafna, and Adam went with Fareed to Gulmarg, a scenic town in the foothills outside of Srinagar. I had a quiet day at home except for listening to wood being sawn, like a drone, all day. I valued a day to myself sometimes. I had grown up in a busy family home so having the house to myself occasionally was a treat. I needed a day at home to get some things done. I was reading, washing and packing for our hike to the glacier.

I was also drawing. I was trying to free up my line, to break out of stylistic rigidness that had been in my work for a while. I would just scribble in the corner and turn the pages and let myself be careless. The drawings didn't look like anything, no need for images and objects in this series, just a line. I divided the page roughly in half, made a format, and drew running back and forth, up-and-down. I was also really into studying the landscape and its horizon.

At lunch Omar asked if I would I like to go to the Hazratbal Mosque again with Aliya and the girls. Today was a special day. There would be an event like a bazaar or fair, with many stalls all around the mosque. The trip would take two hours to and from. We would go by shikara with Granny, Aliya, Nasser, Salama, Aliya's sister and her baby girl, and a few other young girls. Omar's nephew Hadar would be rowing. Of course I would go and thanked him.

The shikara was jammed full with no space between everyone. We were constantly hanging on, leaning on each other in order to stay comfortable and upright. I felt somehow comforted by their acceptance and inclusion of me. I missed hugs and kisses. The children would even hold the granny's earlobes and face in their hands. We would have hands on each other's shoulders, locked tight, especially when the boat moved out into the busy water where many shikaras were heading for the mosque. It was a kind and caring collective energy, which I loved.

My legs were straight in the boat while many others were balled up, as I couldn't sit for a long time like that. I was kindly served first when we ate tea and bread in the boat. People from other shikaras looked in at me. I felt conspicuous, with a simple shirt that looked like a man's and white pants with short hair, no jewellery, and a borrowed scarf.

As we got nearer to the mosque, I remembered some recurring dreams I had before this trip. This was not a *déjà vu* experience but the place looked similar to the dreams and so felt familiar. There was a similar scene, people and a view of the mountains.

Some people were now sleeping on our boat. Aliya and Granny mouthed words to each other silently, so as not to wake the children. On arriving at the mosque area, some of the younger ones woke and began wailing and crying anyhow.

We parked the boat on the far side of the site. We walked back past the mosque and bought some dhal, red beans, toasted rice, and curry. We ate it there and walked to the markets. They bought earrings and bangles for the girls, and scarves for all the mums. We also bought big breads in a basket, lassis, lotus roots in batter, and more bread, tea, and dhal for on the way home.

It was dark by the time we got back to the houseboat at about 9:30 p.m. It had been a good day, as I felt accepted and part of the group. I felt a lot more relaxed and confident being in a foreign country, yet still practically a stranger to them without the same language.

Ryan said his day had been a drag as he was on the bus riding to and from Gulmarg for a long time each way. I had blitzed him on the fun spectrum that day but then he wouldn't have wanted to come with us anyhow.

We spread out and slept on the roof in our sleeping bags and with Fareed curled up in blankets nearby. Ryan said he was planning to wake me early to go to a temple with him and some of the others but I didn't want to go. I was going to do a fast day. We were going to have lunch at 4 p.m. at a Muslim wedding so I fasted until then.

The wedding was held in the manicured gardens of a large beautiful formal home in a very upmarket area of Srinagar. Outside there were many rows of big round stainless steel cooking pots with lids outside on the grass. The women were in a divided off section of a huge outdoor marquee and looked through holes in the walls of hanging fabric at the men on the other side. The floors in the house and the marquees were all covered in rugs. I felt quite under-dressed so stayed in the background. There were speeches and rows of distinguished guests under the marquee and we sat outside on chairs in the back row.

After a long day we ended up at Omar's brother's hotel where we had a supper of tea and lassi, cooked apricots, cabbage and rice, cauliflower, potatoes and vegetables. Everyone played cards and I slept for a short while in the lounge. I woke up suddenly. I talked to Ryan about my dreams of being back at our art school with the drawing lecturer, in a life drawing class. It seemed really odd bringing an old experience into this new world that we were in. Dreams and memories are weird sometimes. I think I was missing my art practice.

The next day we had a random idea that after India we might go to Italy, to eat some pizza and pasta. This probably wouldn't happen, as we hadn't even gotten out of Kashmir yet.

Ryan had bought four new books while I was still finishing *The Agony and the Ecstasy*. The next book I wanted to borrow was Andre Gide's *Fruits of The Earth* from another traveller, Mick, who said he would be finished on Sunday. He recommended it but qualified it as a "giddy" book. Ryan was reading Camus, and then shaved Mick's head. I was drawing.

Trek to the Kolahoi Glacier

THE NEXT DAY we headed off on our trek to Sonamarg, a hill station, and on to the Mount Kolahoi Glacier. I had the same breakfast that I had had for two weeks: hot fresh Kashmiri flatbread and butter, and Persian white tea.

We got on the bus at 8 a.m. running to catch it carrying our packs. I sat next to a man with a red hat like a turban. This was not wound as the Sikhs wear them but a constructed hat that just sat on his head.

Then we caught another bus at 9:30 a.m. to Pahalgam and walked to the camp via a swinging pedestrian bridge, over rocky paths, passing many mules and locals.

The next day we walked ten miles to get to the glacier base camp. The river camp was about 9,000 feet above sea level. The top areas of the glacier averaged more than 14,000 feet with the peak 17,800 feet. Many treks in Kashmir started out of Pahalgam. I took photos of the hill slopes and valleys behind us, and of a pony, that ran off from our group on a windy spur.

It dawned on me that we were walking into what looked like Switzerland. There were bright green rolling hills and distant snowy alpine slopes. It was postcard perfect visual bliss and took my breath away. It was so beautiful. The air was pristine with a crisp breeze. The water in the streams was clean and chilled for drinking. It was silent. There were smaller rolling green hills and soft light green valleys. There was a stunning snow bridge.

Trekking in the hills.

The glacier area.

Walking closer to the glacier.

We took turns riding two small horses. The altitude made us spacey. I watched Ryan riding like a professional. Some people were galloping. I thought I was walking fast but apparently the altitude was slowing me down so I rode a horse for a while. There were still mountain people riding past.

The weather was pleasant and sunny during the day but very cold at night. I had woollen socks, a woollen jumper and a Japara coat that I slept in.

We stopped for snacks for energy going up the mountain. We drank coffee with cornflakes and chocolate condensed milk.

That night I led a few of us to find a stream of the river to wash my socks and ourselves. The refrigeration method they used was hanging food on tree branches overnight in the cold. I drank a lot of lime water and tea.

The next morning I woke up with the singing of a bird that resembled a nightingale's sound. In my morning meditation I was smiling and nearly crying remembering all the beauty of the last day. It was hard to imagine going back home too soon.

I was really improving in fitness due to all the walking. I was looking at the gypsy people. Their ponies had many blankets or rugs on their backs. The women were petite and angular with strong faces. They wore embroidered caps, brightly patterned clothing and plastic shoes with clip fasteners. They wore their hair in many plaits, loosely looped or caught up at the back and were often carrying babies. No women had short hair like me. They stopped sometimes and stared at me.

One gypsy woman waved to get us out of the way. She was standing very straight and erect. She was stunningly powerful, dignified and graceful as she walked.

The gypsy men were twice her size and very handsome with dark beards and eyes, slender in their baggy trousers. Their heads and bodies were wrapped up in large woollen blankets, which fell from the shoulders in a wide expansive curve, as they walked with slow, strong gaits.

There were also goats, sheep, cattle, water buffalo, horses, small beautiful black camels, baby donkeys, and a camel of a most glorious sienna colour. I saw multicoloured mushrooms growing in moist, treed areas.

It had been a wonderful trek following these mountain paths and walkways and sharing them with such strong resilient people. I felt like Alice in Wonderland. The glacial mountains ahead were stunningly beautiful. I touched Ryan's face to get his attention and we shared a moment of awe. Ryan and I were united in this blissful place. Any frustrations we had about each other were irrelevant. We understood each other's need for beauty and freedom in those moments.

I was drinking a lot of coffee, which reminded me of a couple of years ago when I drank it like water, black with sugar. I could not completely give up coffee even though it made me really speedy.

A horseman rode past in what looked like red stripy pyjamas and a grey poncho while singing like a bulbul, a small singing bird here. It was a bit like, "Tweet, tweet, ta, tweet, ta, tweet." He galloped off up the hill on hard ground. He was really lean, and stood up in the stirrups. He patted the horse and said, "good girl," resting his arm on her mane.

Omar wanted me to stay with the other girls Anna and Dafna, at our base camp and not go up on the glacier. They were fine with that but I was not. He spoke about the unstable moving rocks that sat on the soft ice and soil. I thought, *You've got to be kidding me!* Somehow I talked him into letting me go. I looked seriously at him but smiled inside for joy.

Tomorrow would be an early morning to get up and go to the glacier. I decided I must get a mountain goat postcard after this. I checked out my feet to see if I had any blisters. They were soft, white, and fleshy and the soles of my shoes were slightly pitted. There was a four-day-old Elastoplast covering old blisters that were in the damp, slightly soggy corners of my recently washed thick hiking socks. I did not feel like Alice in Wonderland anymore.

My hands looked stronger than they used to. The skin was tougher and browner with small blonde hairs. There was a crack on the inside of my thumb that was not there before. I curled my fingers up to warm them inside the sleeves of my woollen jumper. I had a few random thoughts. *Does it matter where I am? My family don't know. Should I be anxious about going up on the glacier?* I saw trees reflected in my coffee.

I was up at 5:30 a.m. the next day. There was a crescent moon. The land around us was so green with mushy snow in heaps. As I moved around I woke Fareed, who had been sleeping next to the ashes of last night's fire.

The drinking water was a slightly brown colour with some froth on top.

Today we must walk eight miles each way. For the last mile we must leave the ponies and go up to the top of the rocks, approximately 4,000 feet up. I was excited, full of adrenalin, and couldn't wait to try to meet the challenge. I tried not to think about any doubts I might dig up about it.

At 7:45 a.m. we headed off to the Kolahoi Glacier. At 10:30 a.m. we stopped for a small meal at a tent house near a river, with a rock wall around it.

We had to cross this river to get to the glacier. As we walked up the hill towards the river crossing there were small streams of water trickling through boulders. The rocks moved underfoot. This river was shallow in the morning but apparently each evening it would swell from the snow melting off the glacier.

As we walked upwards away from the valleys, I was slowing down perhaps due to the lack of oxygen. It was easier to traverse the areas where it levelled out. At last we went up on the glacier, walking along powdery ledges with two guide ropes at times.

We walked over rocks, snow and dirty, dusty, paths and I picked up ice to hold in my hand that would not melt, as it was so cold. I saw faults and breaks in the snow and the ice, but Omar and his team knew where to walk. I was nervous at times. It sometimes came in the form of a slow wave of concern and at other times as a lightning quick panicked thought. I kept it to myself and followed instructions. Anxiety was a luxury I had no time for. I was not really a big risk taker at home so this was stretching me.

Crossing over large snow covered rock bridges amidst the towering slopes, the sound and sight of water rushing underneath us was pretty and intensely exciting. Some melted snow streams were green and grey while others were white and frothy. It took us about four and a half hours to get up fully onto the glacier. We walked on its blinding expanse and then sat to look around at the surrounding majestic rocky peaks.

I felt my energy was directly related to the unique atmosphere on this mountaintop. As I breathed in, it gave me energy. I felt so healthy and fit, as if the intensely fresh air was powering my movements. I felt so euphoric, being single and free to travel like this.

We spent quite some time basking in the sun on the snowy glacier, on the top of the world surrounded by the mountains. The extended views were breathtaking. It was a very special time. I took photos as we approached the glacier but once we got on to the glacier I forgot to take any more photos.

The scenery was blindingly stunning with mountains all around us. It felt like the top of the world. I wanted more experiences like this. This is why I was travelling.

At 12:30 p.m. we headed down from the glacier, though I would have rather stayed a little longer. We were going downhill with gravity but it would take us five hours to get back to the camp where we had left the others. Walking down from the glacier I felt some kind of indigestion or internal pressure. It was not a huge concern but clearly noticeable nonetheless. Was it the altitude?

Omar and some of the men were concerned we were taking too long. He had to keep us on a schedule in order to cross the river before it swelled from too much water, as it did every evening from the melting ice and snow from the mountains. Clouds were building over the mountaintops.

As we approached the river crossing spot it was completely different to this morning. It had become a large fast-flowing river. Omar looked around at all the members of our group. We had two brown horses, a few Kashmiri men, two Australian men, Ryan and Tim, one Canadian man, Adam, and myself.

The first to cross the river was a Kashmiri man on horseback who unfurled a thick rope as he went. It was tied to large rocks on the other bank and watched closely by a group of Kashmiri men in large brown shawls wrapped around their bodies and heads.

Then two of the Kashmiri men on our side of the river hung on to each other and the rope, and started to cross the river. They wrestled and pushed back against the water and rocks and helped each other across as a team.

In pairs the men inched their way to the other bank using the rope to guide them. I was nervous about how I would do this.

Omar turned to me and gestured me forward. I was to ride the only other horse across the river. I wasn't strong enough to resist the force of the river on my own.

The rocks we had stepped on to come across in the morning were now dangerously unstable, rolling from time to time in the rapid current. If a rock shifted and hit me it would push me down the river. Again, being anxious or scared was a luxury I could not afford at that moment. I had no choice. I had to do this.

I wasn't a confident rider. I had ridden a donkey down a steep hill a few days ago but I really just held on while someone else whacked its rump and told it to go. I don't think I would call that riding.

As I was helped up on to the horse, Omar looked into my eyes and said, "Have no hesitation" and very seriously gave me two more instructions that he then repeated to make sure I had them. He told me, "Hold on to the guide rope with your left hand...*it is your life.*" The second was to only put my feet halfway into the stirrups. "If the horse goes down, pull your feet out of the stirrups and hang on to the rope. We will pull you in."

I realised how serious this was. I realised they weren't that sure that I would get across. I was much shorter than everyone in our group. On the other side of the river a group of Kashmiri mountain people were now gathering to watch. They looked as if they weren't sure about me either. I could see their dark eyes under their shawls. I felt sober and really on high alert. I had no choice. I could not stay on the glacier overnight. I could not consider the consequences; I just went. I trusted Omar's call.

So the horse, with me as its passenger, stepped slowly out into the river. I held the guide rope in my left hand and its reins in my right hand. Every step the horse took I felt deeply. The water deepened as we moved forward. Sometimes my mount hesitated as she walked and the waves crashed around us.

About halfway across the river, the water was up to the horse's neck. There were crashing white rapids and a flow of deeper green water all around us. I felt as if we were pinned there by the pressure that we pushed against. My heart was racing. I had to keep it together. The water was covering my legs and was nearly to my waist. My two hands were still gripping the rope and reins, while my feet were still halfway into the stirrups.

Then the horse's front legs crumbled underneath her. Her face was still just out the water as she stretched her head and neck upwards to breathe. Her right eye and I had connected.

As we watched each other, time stood still. I had no thoughts. I sat extremely still. I was frozen, looking into her eye. In my peripheral vision I could see she was kneeling. I said nothing and I did nothing. I just remained really calm. I was going to see this out because I was not getting off that horse! It was both very noisy but also completely silent sitting there. It was a dynamic experience but also a completely still and timeless period.

After what seemed like a long time the horse brought up one leg. After a little more time, she brought up the other. She stood, and then stood a while longer, remaining still for a few moments to gain her composure. Then she stepped gingerly and very slowly walked forward, almost stumbling again, but strongly pushing her body back against the current. Step-by-step, we made it. As we reached the shallow water on the other side of the river, I swung my leg over her and slid off. I let her run on ahead of me to the riverbank, while I followed on cold, wet, and shaking legs.

The Kashmiris looked at me and then dispersed. I looked at them and then turned to look back across the river at the few remaining men to come. No one said anything. I think they were amazed I made it and I felt quite proud of my achievement. I felt exhilarated. There were a lot of dark eyes that darted around to find other things to watch. The next two men began to cross holding the rope. I just stood there subtly trembling.

We had a half-hour stop for everyone to rest after that treacherous river crossing. We had tea there at the tent camp surrounded by a stacked stonewall, while people collected themselves and dried their clothes a bit near fires. Then we walked on. It took us an hour and a half to go three miles after that.

The camp after crossing the river.

The camp after crossing the river.

I had gained confidence with the horse that helped me over the water and rocks, so I rode her some more, as I had lost one of my shoes during the river crossing. I had slip-on latex shoes in my pack that I would get out back at camp to walk home in.

At 3:30 p.m. we ate lunch after crossing three wooden plank bridges and a large fallen tree. I felt incredibly hungry and my adrenals were surging so I ate anything and everything including Ryan's leftovers. I drank many glasses of water and did deep breathing.

Maybe it was the coffee but for the next two or three miles I ran downhill while chatting with Fareed. I told him I thought I wanted to remain single, at least in my twenties, as I wanted to travel and I couldn't find anyone I liked. He said he didn't want to get married either. He said it was bad after you got married, as there was a lot of fighting. His father would choose who he married as he didn't want to. He didn't want to get old either and would prefer to go into the hills and be like a hippie and "Take it as it comes."

I was distracted and found a little insect in my underwear, which I removed by squashing it and letting it drop out my trouser leg.

When we got back to the campsite called Lidderwat I borrowed Adam's jacket to keep warm. I was sitting under a tarpaulin made into a tent like a pyramid of blue plastic. The bridge of my nose was badly sunburnt.

I moved away from the boys who were playing cards and read Gide and meditated in my tent. I watched a very fast walking insect cross the ground. I ate a couple of glucose biscuits, dipping them in black coffee that already had two sugars. I was getting my energy back after the day's hiking.

Ryan was galloping a horse across a large green expanse between the tree-lined hills. He lost a blanket from the horse so we all wandered around, looking for it and eventually found it.

This Lidderwat camp was where the other trekkers had rested while we had gone up on the glacier. There was a lot of talk among the Kashmiri team who had come up the glacier with us, and those who had not come up. It was about how, "Australian women can walk." I was resting, reading a book and getting way too much attention from two of those horsemen. I was the only woman who had gone so they were all clearly talking about me. Yes, I did feel a bit vain and proud, but it reminded me of wolf whistles from a building site. At some point you don't like the attention.

The next day we were walking upwards again, to Tarsar Lake, which was near the range of the glacier we had trekked. At the end of this track, you had to hike up a steep hill to the lake in the crater at the top. Adam and I stopped further down, as we were spent from yesterday's glacier hike. Ryan, Omar, and the red striped pyjama man walked on. Their photos of the flat, turquoise, pristine, heavenly lake looked amazing.

Then the next day was a fifteen-mile walk to Pahalgam. We had lunch with tea by a stream at Aru. We walked from 9:30 a.m. until noon, and again from 1 p.m. until 4 p.m. I had a stimulating, almost heated talk with Ryan. I had no idea why he kept challenging me on my meditation. He was clearly trying to work out something in himself and it annoyed him that I was reasonably happy with what I was doing. He was doing most of the talking. I was feeling deeply relaxed after such an amazing few days and was really just putting up with him.

We discussed my personality faults that he thought probably were affecting him, as we were all of a sudden spending a lot of time and many experiences together. I thought we were just very different and I didn't really care. He listed my faults as vagueness, indecisiveness, and maybe some fears, due to lack of experience. Looking back, he was probably accurate in his assessment but I had other more positive traits too. I have always been a bit hyperactive and nervous but on the other side I felt quite together, determined and capable. I just didn't talk all the time. I liked Ryan and I might have become closer to him but about that I was indeed being indecisive.

I became stressed at times hanging out with Ryan. Was there innuendo here? Was he talking about us as a couple again? Did he think I was too vague and indecisive about him? Was I not experienced enough for him? Is that why he was so intense when he talked about our friendship? Did he want more? Maybe I was a bit thick.

The next day we caught the bus home. We had a porter who carried baskets and hessian bags with some food and things we needed. Everyone returning to the houseboat felt transformed from the trek. We were all on an emotional *high*. I felt refreshed mentally and emotionally.

There was another new doonga in the canal opposite the Emperor's Palace. Nothing stays the same.

Heading South

THE NEXT DAY I had a picnic with Tim and Anna. We decided to go down into India in about ten days after resting up from the trek. I didn't want to wait for Ryan. After the glacial trek I felt more confident, decisive, and eager for more travel. It had been the transfusion of courage I needed. I had been reading about existentialism and felt I was responsible for my own direction, whereas Ryan had not yet decided what he wanted.

It was hard to explain to Omar why I was going with Anna and Tim. It would be too easy to stay there. Independence was important to me this year. I felt like breaking free from *my new family* as he described himself, Aliya, and the others. Aliya told me she thought my travel was good and was very happy for me. She wanted me to come back again. Inside I knew I wouldn't.

I needed new experiences. I was going away this year without my own *real* family to see lots of new places. Perhaps I felt life at home was pre-determined? I had a strong intuitive pull to leave.

I read about *isotropy,* which was sameness in every direction; any place, time, activity or person was as relevant as any other. Comically I thought my diary was now reading as if I was a travelling philosopher.

Maybe that is what a gap year can be, could be: existentialism. I was twenty-two and a quiet, self-sufficient kind of person. Instead of talking a lot of this stuff out I was thinking about it and noting it in my diary. I didn't feel that I was having an existential crisis, but I was getting in ahead of it with lots of ideas about what people thought about it. I felt content, excited, and also quite anxious as it was stretching my limits a lot.

I read:

Yoga means union,

Castaneda,

Krishnamurti, each individual has the entire universe, nothing else was necessary,

Da Vinci went alone, as with a friend you only had half the experience, by yourself all,

Ulrick, set up a farm then art,

Bentov, *Stalking the Wild Pendulum,*

A black hole was an old universe that goes in and out to a new one,

Matter was decreasing,

Energy goes in the black hole.

Today Ryan and I went with Anna and Tim to buy bus and train tickets to New Delhi. I liked this couple. They seemed very together, had a lot of travel experience, were fun and interesting to talk to. They only smoked dope occasionally and not recently. Ryan bought some more books.

The cupboard door where I was keeping my pack was ajar when I got back. I said nothing about it so emotionally once again I was acting mostly out of consideration for others. Someone or something was mentally draining me. Oscillation, my pendulum was swinging back. I need a bit of isolation. It would be good to write and draw tonight.

Camping and trekking was good, but this family situation was too protective. I wanted to be a single person in the universe again.

Last night I was sleeping on the couch in the living room, with the torn wallpaper. I had an early breakfast. Aliya was sick, and Omar had me read several testimonial letters about his houseboat. Was this his way of trying to convince me to stay?

I bought a canvas board for Ryan as a parting gift to support him to paint again. We ate omelettes, took our malaria tablets and drank chai. He was behaving more politely and gently now that I was leaving and I felt our friendship was warm and healthy. I think my impending departure may have given him the clear signal we were not going to be a couple but I also knew we would miss each other.

I was doing reading lessons with pouting Omar. I met Lena on the houseboat roof. She was a German girl travelling to Canada, and we played cards that night. I was losing concentration but she and her friend Josh were good company. I cooked chapattis tonight with Fareed, as Aliya was sick.

As Dafna and Adam, the American couple, left Srinagar today, I was sleeping alone in a proper room now and hoped to do a full round of asanas, pranayama and meditation in the morning. I was leaving our tent and other equipment with Ryan, so he could sell them or keep using them. I asked him to redirect my mail and gave him my books.

I asked Lena and Josh about beaches to go to in India. I made lists. The next morning Aliya was lying on the grey rug while we all ate porridge and drank chai. Omar was talking about superstitions to himself aloud and worrying about his finances: "Who has crossed us as there was only one rupee in my pocket?"

These people were not my family but they were beginning to demand things, expect things. Omar was worried about the tent and space blanket as if he wanted them. He worried about the Apollo satellite. He said, "We don't treat you as a tourist so you have to do as I say". I felt a bit stressed but threw in some hysterical laughter and silly jokes to try to jolly it all along. I went off to read Patanjali to even out.

I wrote to the YWCA in Delhi for future accommodation. I wrote to my brother and his wife of nearly seven years. He was twenty when he married and she was eighteen, and they have two gorgeous young daughters. I'm not ready yet to do it, though one day I might. I still wanted to go to the museum, art school, and Yusmarg before I headed off.

I was reading about:

Correct spinal posture,

Don Quixote,

And two books by Krishnamurti.

I felt lazy and played cards for a long time in the doonga after breakfast. Aliya gave me two viridian plastic bangles. I began Krishnamurti's *Beyond the Violence*. It encouraged me to think that I was pretty sure I could travel on my own now.

I bought some grapes for our short hike around Srinagar then we sunbaked on a quiet road.

Later I went with Ryan, Omar, and Aliya to the doctor, as she was still unwell. She looked very tired and ill, and we were all a bit worried about her. She was prescribed three strong pills and some pink medicine. They also discussed aluminium hydroxide, bicarbonate of soda, and chlorophyll. Then we went to the passport office.

That night a few of us went to eat with Lena and Josh, our houseboat neighbours next door. They told us about the Vishi Valley near Madras and Krishnamurti. I was learning bridge.

That night Aliya gave me a few more bangles when changing clothes and told me about her earring collection.

The next day I said to Omar that worrying was ruining him and wearing him out. He had begun to meet with us about many things, he was not sleeping, and he wanted five hundred rupees from Ryan and had hinted at it from me too. I wondered what this was for and was suspicious. I had paid all my rent and less when sleeping on the roof.

I found out that his budgeting for the treks was not good and he hadn't made much profit. I actually didn't mind. It was about sixty dollars Australian and clearly it meant a lot to him. He had been an excellent host for my last six weeks in Srinagar so I was happy to pay.

Yusmarg and Back in Srinagar

AT 11 A.M. I caught a bus with Omar, Lena, Josh, and Ryan to Charar-i-Sharief and had tea in a stall at the bus stop there. The crowd getting on and off the bus were very quiet but Lena and I were a bit oblivious, enjoying ourselves, and talking loudly. We discussed things we would do back home. I was planning to throw out lots of things so it would be easier to move house.

From Yusmarg we walked about two miles through pristine vivid green nature to Nilnag Lake. Ryan and Josh would have liked to stay there for a week but the plan was overnight. The kids herding were watching us and not the cows.

The following day I woke early, meditated in my sleeping bag and washed in the toilets. My gut was still playing up so I decided I'd stay in the hut for the day while Ryan, Lena and

Josh rode horses to the Dudhaganga River, a tributary of the Jhelum River.

I wrote to four of my good friends in Melbourne about the possibility of coming home in October and then travelling for a month in Australia, if they were free to come too.

I also talked with Ryan about keeping in touch. We decided to write letters to each other when travelling in case we wanted to meet up.

This Yusmarg area was an alpine hill station in the west of the Kashmir valley about twenty-five miles south of Srinagar. The name Yusmarg means *Meadow of Jesus*. It was believed by a local Muslim community that Jesus came and lived there for some time.

There was a very windy storm with awesome, unusual clouds that had a light aura around them. The wind was wonderful, pushing distant rustling noises through the pine trees, blowing the pine smell everywhere. After the storm the sky looked like a sea with a grey fluffy cloud machine throwing strings of smaller clouds.

Josh and Lena were back from riding up the Dudhaganga and went to play cards. There were two voluptuous women flirting with everyone. Ryan said if I followed the edge of the woods I would get to the river, so I took the Krishnamurti Reader and quietly had a nap there. Later there was another lightning storm. Then we played cards in the shade of a beach umbrella, with radio music and chai.

We walked seven miles past Nilnag Lake. It was a multicoloured fantasyland of crops, super green pine trees, pretty flowering plants, strong tasting wild strawberries, bordered by apricots and pear trees.

As we walked Omar told us the local news that fuelled their anxieties: the Skylab was falling, India was treating Kashmir badly, monsoons brought malaria, and Pakistan, and Afghanistan governments were kept in power by Russian communists.

Last night we all talked about why the Himalayas, though high in good negative ions with rare altitude, had such hostile social and political environments.

Lena and I talked for hours today while walking in stony riverbeds, and soft grey clay streets teeming with chickens, street kids, elderly ladies, and schoolchildren. A smiling woman selling yellow maize bread spoke to Omar about us as she thought we were nice girls and then gave us a free loaf. I divided the free bread to share and there was lots of calling out from our group of "You gave Ryan more than us!"

Lena and Josh climbed up a grass bank and found really dusty sheep that felt soft like talc. We followed them over a ridge, surrounded by wheat fields with people in vibrant coloured clothing harvesting. There were large bundles of wheat, cattle, and kids, and large trees to shade the workers. Omar saw a passing bus that Ryan ran ahead to catch but it escaped.

We stopped on this dusty track and I looked at my filthy feet. Half of my blisters on the left heel were from trekking the Kolahoi Glacier. They reminded me of a great time and I was quite proud of them. We walked into a small town that had electricity lines but no shops, followed by many families with babies.

We saw a teacher walking kids in a line to the bus stop. We piled on to the Srinagar bus with lots of children. One put her tired head down to doze on Josh's sleeping bag. We saw a *Chess Match* sign hanging on a porch.

I sat in the back seat with Ryan, Josh and two other men. There was little room so we held all our packs on our laps. There was a woman in a stunning green sari nearby, who I chatted with. Her sari cost two hundred and forty rupees and was made from Georgette fabric from the U.S.A. She said that we travelled here for enjoyment but for her it was living hell to take the bus and walk. She said there was no work in the hills and most of her family lived in Srinagar. It was a good, smooth ride, past rice paddies and green countryside. We talked about all the different shades of green we could see in the lush vegetation. We could have talked all day and I was up for it as my family have the talking gene. I really enjoyed her company. Sometimes a stranger can be fun.

Back at the Emperor's Palace, Aliya was eating raw string beans as we walked in. She really needed to eat cooked food like us to keep well, as the doctor suggested. They said a Muslim grace over the meal, which I hadn't seen before, maybe because the grandmother was there.

After dinner on the houseboat a few people wanted to go to the beer shop. I was mucking around and splashing some of the others in the shikara. It became a little rowdy so I was let off to stay back. I didn't want any booze anyhow.

There was a beautiful moon so I sat up on the roof and decided to sleep there. I heard people coughing and spitting in preparation for sleep.

I woke to a misty, sunny morning around 6:30 a.m. I would miss this place that had become so familiar. And then I fell asleep again.

The next day I went with Anna, Tim, Lena, and Josh to the old city area of Srinagar for a horse and cart ride along cobblestone streets. Ryan stayed home to have a haircut. My hair had started growing back but I didn't want a trim. I would let it grow out. We saw copper shops then walked around the mosque and old town. We shared a litre of lassi at a shop.

On the way back we met Ryan and Omar. I finalised what my final large payment with Omar would be. He was more relaxed then. Later in the lounge room I felt freer and less obligated. Everyone was calm until Fareed talked about the end of the world that would happen in three months after the upcoming Ramadan.

I was learning the game Mastermind while I sewed the cloth cover on a parcel before posting. I listened to the *Skylab was falling* conversations and various other sky superstitions. The Skylab would touch down at 9:30 p.m. Most of Omar's family thought it would crash here on top of us in Kashmir. We listened to Radio BBC, London from 8:45 p.m. They announced that in two minutes it would land in Africa. In reality it shattered in the Western Australia desert.

Anxious conversations shifted back to Ramadan. It was quite stressful being here at the moment. I remembered the book *Beyond the Violence* about just being with thoughts and observing them, aware without judgement. I was putting on weight and learning not to react to chubby jokes. I was aware I was writing nonsense and glad to be heading off.

I slept in the back room on my open cotton sleeping bag. In the morning I meditated, had a bucket shower, then ate with Ryan and two people from Sydney, John and Sharon, who arrived with their packs.

The new people asked me about T.M. versus drugs. I said drugs dulled the mind and that T.M. woke it up. They reacted strongly, saying maybe I jumped out of religion into T.M. Fine by me.

Another new tourist, Imrin, arrived and provided desserts and biscuits for a party planned for later as Anna, Tim, and I were leaving. We went to the shops for drinks and there we spoke with a sheik about the Skylab. I had a spider on my shirt and Tim kept telling me there were more. He kept startling me but it was funny.

There were storm clouds early this morning; white and blue then soft deep greys that were changing the colour of the hills below them. I sunbaked on the roof as it might be my last chance for a while.

I sometimes notice my polite and insecure laugh. I'm working on getting rid of that. I'm trying to watch my reactions to things.

Today I also visited an art school in Srinagar. I took a local bus but didn't note down details of the college name or whereabouts in my diary. I instantly felt at home. It was small but the intent of the place; the art materials, their smell, and the quite relaxed openness of conversation were so familiar. The students worked in groups on the same projects, such as, a still life. I had considered trying to stay here or somewhere else in India by teaching art but learnt from this experience that there were not many jobs or students.

The next day I went to the city with Ryan to Ahdoo's hotel restaurant, opened in 1918 and still there for fine dining in the Kashmir Valley. It was a quiet and meaningful time together before we were to split up. We talked a lot about how he was also here travelling to study himself. I really enjoyed this self-reflective time with him. We were happy taking this time out from the houseboat to acknowledge our friendship and experiences so far. We had struggled at times but now swum around in our warm and fuzzy friendship.

I Left Kashmir But Ryan Stayed

THE NEXT MORNING I was up early at 5:30 a.m. to dress and get ready. It was the 15th of July so I had spent fifty-one days in Kashmir. I found Fareed, Aliya, and Omar. I didn't want my usual chai and then woke Ryan. He and Josh were now sleeping outside of the houseboat in two doongas moored to it. Josh poked just his head out of his doonga. Ryan had been deeply asleep before I woke him. He had irritated red eyes. As he was trying to wake up he nearly tipped over his doonga. I kissed his hairy cheek.

As Anna, Tim and I left, I waved back at them all a few times. There were no waves back from Ryan, only just the simple words, "Take care of yourself." I replied with "Don't fall off a mountain." It was restrained but an intensely emotional parting. We had nothing left to say. I tried not to panic about leaving my only familiar reference point in Ryan. I hoped we'd meet up again in a few months.

Fareed rowed over for a handshake, then looked back as he rowed off. I was nearly crying and did later on the bus. I had been in Kashmir nearly two months but glad to be on my way. I felt I had grown up a bit there and had experienced support from some very good people in a foreign country. This gave me great confidence to travel more. There might be danger but there might also be good things.

We bussed it to Jammu and I saw a few last picturesque views of the stunning hills.

At the train station we checked in at an island desk then sat with others until boarding time. Everyone called Tim, "Mr. Tim." On the train I sat next to a quiet man in a blue shirt with three little boys. After a sleep on the top bunk I sat to read and watch people get on and off at all the small local stations.

PART 2

**South into India, Sri Lanka
and Back to India**

Delhi, Agra, Bombay, Ajanta and Ellora

I TRAVELLED SOUTHWARDS with Anna and Tim. When we arrived in a new place, we often stayed in the same accommodation but went our separate ways during the day. I was aware I was a third wheel, though nothing was ever directly stated. I was happy to give them space and at times to be on my own too. It would have been great to travel with a partner but I didn't have one, obviously! They had been travelling overland, seemed tired and got a bit short with each other sometimes. Anna and I chatted a lot so I was a distraction. We hadn't discussed how long I would travel with them.

We travelled by bus to Agra, a much smaller city than Delhi. I had to close my eyes at times as the driver repeatedly just missed other vehicles. The air was less polluted there and the speed of life was less overwhelming and dominating.

I went to see the Taj Mahal several times. The first visit blew my mind, as it was so stunningly majestic in such a peaceful, lush, and manicured garden setting. There was a small entrance fee, but no long queues; there was hardly anyone there.

I would walk around enjoying the extreme beauty, poetry, orderliness and tranquillity of the building and acres of gardens. It stood out in contrast to any other buildings I had seen as yet, a luxurious place in the middle of a densely populated country. It recharged me. I would take a book and sit on the grass under the trees and sometimes doze in the warmth and peace with my back supported by the trunk of a tree. I did not want to lie down and completely fall asleep on my own.

One time I was under the trees on a sunny idyllic day, reading Maharishi Mahesh Yogi's translation and commentary on the Bhagavad Gita. The book is an ancient Sanskrit text, written down about 400 BCE. It was a seven hundred-verse conversation between Arjuna, a warrior preparing for battle, and Krishna, his charioteer and part of the epic Mahabharata. I had been reading it for some time and was engrossed in it.

I hadn't noticed that very quietly about twenty Saddhus had sat down under the same trees and encircled me. I then became aware of it and looked around at this group of men with very long dreadlocks, orange clothing and tikka-covered foreheads. I wondered what was going on. I felt a little awkward and bewildered.

One younger Saddhu stood up in front of me and spoke to me in English. He said something like "Could you tell us something about the Gita?" As I looked around the group and back at him, he repeated the request. I felt ill-equipped to tell them what I knew about the Gita. I felt deep respect for these religious ascetics and just quietly got up nodding and saying "Namaste" as I went out of the gardens. I was too shy to know what to do. In hindsight I could have just read something from the book, as it had a very good commentary on each verse.

Next we went to Bombay. We arrived by train and it was raining. With our backpacks on, and in the rain, we trudged from hotel to hostel, to eventually find 2 vacant rooms near the station. Tim was pretty flustered.

I liked the way everyone crossed the road there. Even in peak time at the large roundabout opposite the train station you could make the five lanes of bumper-to-bumper car traffic stop for you to cross. I watched the locals and then tried it myself. It was so easy. You stepped up to the curb ready to cross and thrust out your arm straight ahead, raised it and then dropped it, waving your arm like a flag starting a car race. One confident arm wave and all the traffic slammed on their brakes and you walked across. So I learnt to watch what the locals did in any place for this and other things.

We travelled from Bombay inland to the south and Kerala coast. Before we went, we took a day trip by bus to visit the

Ajanta and Ellora caves, UNESCO world heritage sites. The area on approach was mildly undulating and covered in vegetation. Then you walked closer and you saw huge dugouts in the ground where there were layers of buildings descending into the earth, erected over the centuries one on top of the other.

There were about thirty breathtaking ancient rock Buddhist temples that you could step down into. With each step down you were going back in time. The temples were monumental in size and contained massive statues of Buddha. The Ajanta Caves are dated from about 200 BCE to 500 CE. The nearby Ellora caves were from about 500 to 1000 CE and contained also Hindu and Jain temples.

Buddha statues.

Very large lying Buddha statue.

Temple decoration.

There was a great silence in this land away from towns and cities. It was very moving to be there. As our bus circled around in the car park to leave, I was in awe from what I had seen; I was mentally and poetically drunk.

As I daydreamed I looked out of my bus window into the distance. There were not many people around. The car park was just dirt with no crushed stones or other surfaces to control the dust from tyres. I saw several women squatting and sweeping. I wondered why they were sweeping there. Perhaps there was rubbish to sweep up or to control the excess loose dust? Was it to make a shiny surface for tourists? I had seen homes with compressed and shiny mud floors perhaps due to sweeping and walking barefoot.

My attention went to one woman squatting and lightly sweeping in half circles in front of her with a hand broom made of grasses bound together. She patiently, steadily, and rhythmically stepped though squatting. She swept, and stepped and then swept and stepped, and for a moment it seemed timeless.

I was learning, and continue to learn, not to romanticise the beauty I saw in India. There was a romance that was possibly due to the great spirituality of the people I met and places I visited. There was also the achievement that such a large population existed at all as a nation, but there was so much poverty, class divisions, and disparity. I was also aware that the greatness of most past cultures and the incredible buildings and towns that remain for us to visit were made on the back of lower classes or slavery.

But I did see in this woman a breathtaking beauty in mundane action. My grandfather had been a trade union leader. My family believed in equality, workers' rights, human rights, and this had strongly influenced me. The daily grit of workers to just keep going even with a baby tied on your back was awe-inspiring to me. Watching this woman I felt young, naïve, middle class, and ignorant. I was on my gap year whimsically travelling. She was working hard to earn a meagre living.

Not Goa, then Ooty, Bangalore, and Mysore

WE WENT TO several well-known towns and cities in central India. I was excited to pick up the pace, to be moving faster along. I was gaining courage to do more and meet more people along the way. I was looking for some kind of freedom in myself.

We decided not to get off the train at Goa. Many hippies did get off there as this was known as a drug and party town for travellers. I looked at the crowds alighting. It was always a safety issue for me. Decisions in my mind were pretty straightforward though I may not have voiced them much. I really did not want to get off there.

We went to Ooty (or Ootacamund), a hill station popular during the hot months. On the historic steam train, with brightly painted quaint carriages, we slowly headed up into the hills. The vegetation became lush and green while the air became damp, as if entering a cloud. Arriving at the train station was memorable. It was very neat with well-painted station buildings, little white picket fences, and rows of very tidy geranium pots. It was like a proclamation of welcome.

I remember staying in a large dark wood panelled gracious home that had been turned into the YWCA guest house - or was it another guest house on the YWCA Road? It was nestled up into a hill with views of the Ooty village below. The air was fresh, rooms were comfy and clean, and the deep-fried potato chips were amazing with chunky crystals of salt. The menu there was a respite from only eating curries.

I felt really happy here. I enjoyed walking around the hills, into the exotic, slightly overgrown, lush botanical gardens nearby and down into the market area of town. There were also some impressive Christian churches and government buildings along with dense forests.

In the market I bought a black umbrella with a shiny wooden handle for the soft steady rain, which doubled as a walking stick. Later someone told me that I had bought a grandfather's umbrella. Perhaps this design gravitas added to my confidence, as a psychological support; my message was *don't mess with me*. It may also have looked culturally discordant.

Bangalore (now Bengaluru) I knew as a silk producing city but it was so much more than that. It was the capital of the state of Karnataka and seemed like a growth centre for businesses. Everyone we spoke with in restaurants ran their own businesses and spoke positively about Bangalore's future and growth. The education system, schools and colleges, was expanding. The slums were growing due to people moving there to get an education. I believed this hype. Looking out my hotel window I was over the central roundabout where car traffic mixed madly with tuk-tuks, motorbikes, bicycles, and animal-drawn carts.

This city was large with several million people and was an introduction to south India. The weather was tropical now which meant heat and humidity that did slow you down a bit. Since water wasn't always available I was in the habit of drinking chai now. It was readily available, cheap, and kept you going.

Most of the locals were vegetarian, and I was told there were about a thousand Hindu temples with ornately decorated tall tower entrances. Someshwara Temple was about 950 years old and Begur Nageshwara even older. Bangalore was known as a multi-faith place with also many mosques, churches and other places to worship.

While wandering around the city I found that the spruikers outside restaurants had great comedy routines. They were exaggerating how great their food was. In one restaurant I spoke with a traditional Brahmin man. He was from that highest caste in the Hindu religion though not an active priest at that moment. He *saw* me as an Indian and referred to one of my past lives.

On the 31st of July I was in Mysore. This city was different, calmer, and smaller than Bangalore with a central pink, opulent palace. It felt a bit like Australia's capital city Canberra.

Cochin and Trivandrum

MOVING DOWN TOWARDS Kerala the towns and coastline were more tropical, the weather warmer and more humid. The jungle was less dense with more palm trees and fresher air. The sea views reminded me of Australia. Monsoons seemed to be everywhere. Cochin felt like a seaside resort town. The architecture was a combination of British, Dutch, and Portuguese colonialism seen in palaces, government buildings, temples, synagogues, churches, and basilicas. Some were blindingly white-washed.

We then travelled on a motorised long wooden ferry between Cochin and Trivandrum. It was painted a light blue, smelt of diesel fumes and put-put-putted along, stopping regularly to pick up and drop off local people. Many carried parcels, boxes, bags, and an occasional small animal. It travelled along the waterway inside of an atoll that divided the Indian mainland from the surf coast of the Arabian Sea.

Fort Kochi, an area in Cochin, was a visual standout near the beach full of large Chinese fishing nets, colonial markets, and other brightly coloured homes, and markets. It had been a port for centuries and had diverse churches and temples. I felt as if I was moving back in time to colonial then ancient times. I was reminded at times of our diverse and even more ancient cultures in Australia. This place felt as if so many people had been through here and left their mark.

Travelling inside the canal down through Kerala.

Travelling inside the canal down through Kerala.

On the 7th of August I cashed a traveller's cheque at the State Bank of South India, Ernakulam, the central district of Cochin. Then I went to an afternoon of *Traditional Dance Arts of Kerala* at the Theosophical Society Hall in the area. I arrived early as I was told I would be able to watch the dancers dress into their costumes and makeup. I sat near the front with a few families with children and this pre-show included a demonstration of each style of dance. Later when watching the show I knew the meaning of some steps and poses. Most people there spoke some English at times to help me as well.

Their facial expressions were a main part of their work. They put some seeds or juice in their eyes to make the veins stand out as a strong red. On their faces they had put oil and then layers of paint including black as a background, red dots and white lines. The hall filled, the stunning, hypnotic music and dance went for almost three hours.

Trivandrum (now Thiruvananthapuram) was a modern city, the capital of Kerala state. Two health issues came up when there. I was walking along with Anna one day and she told me about an ugly ulcer growing on one of her shins. She had been treating it with creams from the chemists for two or three weeks but it was not clearing up. She was concerned they may have to fly home instead of spending another few months in Asia. I was pretty worried for her as from the brief glimpse I had it looked terrible. She needed to get this fixed and soon.

I mentioned that I had been using an Ayurvedic soap called Chandrika that was readily available and seemed to clear up rashes and cuts pretty well. Its information sheet suggested lathering the soap and spreading this frothy foam on any bad skin problems. You had to leave it on for a few minutes before washing it off. It was a pretty random idea but Anna decided to try it, so we found a shop and bought her some. Several days later she showed me her shin and it had completely cleared up. The infection had dried up, become a scab and peeled off.

We often enjoyed each other's company, but this made me feel useful too!

The second health issue I remember in Trivandrum was that I had diarrhoea for a while now, but I had decided to do something about it. I was managing okay but at times it was uncomfortable. I was walking around the city when I came across a small light blue wooden house with a picket fence around it. On the gate plaque I noticed a symbol that was similar to a homeopathic logo. I am allergic to penicillin so had already used this and other natural doctors back home. I was rapt to find this clinic. So I went inside.

A very dignified older Indian man in a light brown suit indicated to me to take a seat and he sat down opposite me on the other side of his desk. Around him were shelves full of medical books and cabinets of remedies. He looked like the real deal. I thought I was in a good place. He didn't speak English, so I indicated towards my stomach and bottom. He nodded, looked deeply into my face and eyes, and smiled in a knowing way. Tourists frequently got *Delhi Belly* in India, so it wasn't that hard to work out what was going on.

He went into another room and after a few moments brought me back a small glass test-tube bottle with a cork in it. It contained tiny white homeopathic pills. He had long, slender and angular fingers with neatly manicured oval nails. He held up two fingers and then three fingers. So, I said, "two pills, three times per day." He agreed. I took out two pills and sucked them under my tongue. He again nodded. So, I took them and by the same time the next day I had really no symptoms left. I had used homeopathic remedies before and always got quick and good results for colds and digestive issues. Now I knew it worked for diarrhoea too.

Kanyakumari

NEXT WE WERE in Kanyakumari or Cape Comorin, the southernmost tip of India. It is the area where three seas meet: the Arabian Sea, the Indian Sea, and the Bay of Bengal.

There were many fishing boats with a simple canvas sail, which they levered up and down. They would sail out in clusters through the whitewash of surf and come back in intermittently later in the day. The men would bring in the boats, full of fish in wooden boxes, and pull them up on to the sand.

As they arrived in the shallow water, the men, women, and children would run at the boats to help unload the fish. The men onboard might pass a large fish to children who would run back up to their huts on the beach. There were also some hearty bargaining over prices as they sold the boxes to different bidders. It all happened really quickly.

Fishing boats at Kanyakumari.

Kanyakumari fishing and island temple view.

Kanyakumari people bathing opposite the island temple.

On the beach were groups of old men sewing up massive fishing nets piled around them. Children were the loudest screaming and calling out. I sat for hours watching the fishing village at work and felt quite welcomed to be there.

There was another major activity there to do with this special beach area called Triveni Sangam and a temple island opposite. The beach was itself a sacred place where the large oceans at the tip of India merged and many people came to bathe there. One day I watched as several wooden fishing boats full of men went over and clambered up onto the rocky island where the temple was. It looked very dangerous with the waves constantly crashing but they all made it up safely. I could see them sit and worship in groups.

Women and children who came to this beach opposite the temple island would also wade into the water and worship. Young women and children wore cotton dresses. Older women arrived in smart saris but changed into another more plain or cotton sari to wear into the water. They did this by slipping in the end of one sari as they peeled off the other. Inch by inch the saris would change places, like a magic trick. It was such a continuous and smooth process that I was always slightly shocked that I missed some critical moment when they swapped places. They would then walk down into the water to worship before returning to their bags and then after some towel drying, perform the opposite trick. The wet sari would come off, end up folded in a bag, while the smart sari went back on again.

I really enjoyed sitting on the beach people-watching and felt acknowledged and accepted to be there. People might show me what they were doing even though we couldn't speak. The children might hold up their fish. Just like in Kashmir I felt really comfortable in this place and with the local people, which helped me to not be homesick.

One day as I walked back up from the beach through some huts to the road, I noticed one small house had a brass plaque on the gate that looked like it said something about T.M. The front door was ajar so I knocked.

I was let in by a young guy who showed me the front lecture room where there were lots of pamphlets and books to do with T.M. So I was right. I tried to explain that I also did this meditation, and we smiled and hung out for a while. We couldn't progress much further due to the language barrier but it was a friendly visit. He seemed quite happy to have me there.

When I sat on the beach after that I could always look over and see the roof of this small house so close to this significant beach at the southern tip of India. I felt happy and safe in Kanyakumari.

I got to know this town and its simple layout quite well. I lived in a concrete minimalist cube bungalow on the beachfront, west of the fishing area, on the coast of the Arabian Sea. The bungalow had its own bathroom, a large bed with poles and mosquito nets and a large ceiling fan that made the room extremely cold even though the weather was hot.

Sometimes I would walk out along that more isolated beach to watch people swim. They weren't really going into the water but just played in the shallows. This west coast at Kanyakumari had a large expanse of grey mineral sand. The beach was wide and several miles long. There was a drop off in the sand down to the water where the surf had eroded the beach. It was a wild surf beach that I would not have normally swum in.

The teenage girls would swim in their dresses. The men and boys might just roll up their trousers or fold up their dhotis. They might just stand in the shallows while the children chased each other and screamed. I wore my bikini under my clothes sometimes in case I might venture in but it never seemed quite the right time. I would have looked quite different to everyone else there.

My friends were sleeping in. I liked doing things with them, but I felt I met more people by going around on my own. One morning I was walking along the beach with a towel over my shoulder and I became aware that a man was following me. He may have seen foreigners before in their bathers and wanted to watch, or maybe more, who knows, but I wasn't going to ignore him.

I walked back right up to him and screamed in his face that I didn't like being followed. I took a few steps back and thought that he was leaving but again he followed. I screamed at him again, with a bit more swearing and force. I waved my fist at him. This time it worked and he left, but then so did I.

My annoyance and fear had pumped up my adrenalin. It reminded me of my vulnerability travelling alone and I hated him for stirring that up. It would throw me off for a while. I was furious that I could not have a morning walk without this!

There were large white Mahatma Ghandi statues around the town, and I was told some of his ashes had been scattered in the sea near the temple island. Most of the restaurants were vegetarian.

Kanya Kumari was the goddess and protector of the area. There was a 3,000-year-old temple dedicated to her in red and white painted bricks. There were many places around the town where I felt déjà-vu.

Madurai

THE TOWN OF Madurai was built around the Meenakshi Temple. Both the temple and town planning were built according to the ancient Indian design style of Vastu that aligns everything to the four cardinal points. The temple had four entrances to north, south, east, and west. It had an outer wall with corner towers that were highly decorated with sculptural figures that told traditional Vedic stories.

I was mesmerised by the decoration, the complex internal corridors, and wall structures that led into important spots of the temple and specific deities' shrines. I liked the symmetry within the complex and the plinth structures that gave a solid base. It was very impressive. Innocently, I nearly entered the middle inner temple area when someone questioned whether I was female. I was not allowed any further.

I was worried about leaving my shoes outside, but again they were there when we came back. There were mostly local people there and not many other tourists.

Meenakshi Temple, Madurai.

Colombo Then Kandy

THERE WERE TWO ways to cross the Gulf of Mannar between India and Sri Lanka, by boat or plane. We had decided to try both ways. We would go over by sea and then fly back.

Anna, Tim, and I had fallen into patterns by now. Tim liked to step forward and buy tickets and we brought up the rear. I was still feeling like a third wheel as they were really my acquaintances rather than deep friends. I wondered how much longer we would travel together.

We had to line up to buy tickets early on the wharf in India on the day, and then board a wooden motorboat to take us to a larger boat to travel over to Sri Lanka. Queuing there, as a foreigner, with our own dedicated line was easy, and we only had one bag or backpack each. We stood around on the wharf in the hot sun for a couple of hours with other foreign travellers who were also ready to board.

Queuing, if you were an Indian or Sri Lankan, was a completely different experience altogether. There was so much luggage: piles of bags, bulk food supplies, trunks, boxes, baskets, and animals. This was surrounded by family members to carry it. All this had to go out on a small boat to the larger boat as well.

We were allowed to board first which was easy until we had to climb up ropes to the larger boat. I was wearing my backpack so I tried several times before I was successful in getting over the lip and onboard after a friendly nudge at the end.

The sun was beating down still and it was a relief to be on the boat with a slight breeze but then we had to wait again for a couple of hours to depart. I don't remember ever having been in such a long and complicated line-up of people before. The actual ferry ride was not that long, under an hour. I drank a lot of Limca that day.

Disembarkation was easier. The boat pulled up to a very long wooden wharf called the Talaimannar Pier. Nearby along the beachfront there were rows of mud brick huts with palm branch roofs. I noted it was the 12th of August as I cashed a traveller's cheque for fifty dollars into Sri Lankan rupees on the pier. We got to Colombo after an eight hour train ride. It seemed calmer than India here and less populated.

We visited Kandy, in Sri Lanka's central hill region one day after the elephant festival. We had been unable to get train or bus tickets in time for the festival, and were told that all accommodation would be booked out already. The crowds were gone by the time we arrived. We did see some elephants that still had on their painted decorations albeit without the full spectacle of parade and regalia of coloured coats and seats, which some people showed us in their photos.

On the 20th of August I was at Trincomalee. In this idyllic beach area I split up with Anna and Tim. They wanted to travel as a couple for a while. Tim made a clear announcement as we arrived at a shared bungalow on the beach. The third wheel fell off. I asked Tim would it be okay to leave my backpack there until I had found some accommodation and then I'd come back for it. It was quite heavy.

It was a surprise to suddenly be on my own. I felt a little shocked then emotional but tried to hide it. It was a type of rejection and I had to handle it. I tried to control my anxiety, as I had to work out my next step. In some ways I was fine with it. I had spent most days on my own anyhow. I just needed to sort myself out and put on my big kid pants and depend on myself more instead of following along. I found a hotel to stay in not far from the beach. We agreed to write to each other and possibly meet up somewhere else.

I took long walks on Trincomalee's wide and long beaches under large treed areas for shade. It was a really peaceful holiday place to be.

I spent some time with a cook in one of the beach cafes. I loved the coconut-based sauces in the curries after so much hot food in India and she invited me in to see her cook.

She would crack a coconut on a metal stand that was attached to her wooden kitchen table. She deftly caught its juice with a container. At another point she grated each half of the coconut on the metal stand and collected the shavings in a bowl underneath. When the bowl was full, she covered the white pulpy flesh with water and left it to soak as she worked on the next batch of coconuts.

After soaking the shredded coconut for a while in water she squeezed it with her fingers to wring out more juice from the flesh. The bowl filled up with a second form of quite thick coconut milk. We drank some of each sort of milk to see the difference. She then added these milks to her cooking and let me taste those as well. We were both happy to have each other's company.

Walking along the beach often meant chatting with children who wanted to practice their English and ask me twenty questions. What is your name? Where are you from? Why are you on your own? How old are you? Where are your parents? Are you married etc? Cricket scores? The young ones reminded me of my two young nieces at home. One boy saw some hair on my legs that showed under my lungi sarong. He was fascinated as he said he had never seen hairy legs. I said how normal it was and we chatted about it.

Colombo and Hikkaduwa

A FEW DAYS later, back in Colombo on 22nd August I posted a parcel to Jenny, a friend back home. She had already travelled in Asia and India and had asked me to get her some things, like coffee, two hundred beedies (cigarettes made from rolled up tobacco leaves), and two books. It cost seventy rupees to post. It was great to lighten my pack by posting these off. I had wrapped it all in brown paper, but the post office wrapped it again in calico cloth and then hand sewed the seams. Then they put a melted wax seal on the seam and wrote the address directly onto the fabric.

In Colombo someone suggested I try an avocado. I think I may have heard of them at home but I had never tasted one. So, I bought a really big one with quite a smooth sap green coloured skin. I peeled a section at a time and ate it like an apple. It was cooling, soothing in my stomach, filling, and a good change.

Hikkaduwa was a surfers' paradise south of Colombo. There were stunning palm edged beaches. I would eat large bowls of delicious muesli and freshly made yoghurt for breakfast. This was served up in a casual café, one of a string along the road next to the beach. There were lots of tropical fruits, juices, and fresh coconut curries.

I met Australian surfers who had let their passports expire and lived there. They explained the local community had built up from many years of surfers from around the world visiting or deciding to stay. One said he made and sold one surfboard each month to pay his way. Others ran the cafes. They were not really into travelling much besides to other nearby beaches and thought I was pretty gutsy on my own.

Here I did wear my bikini but kept it covered in a lungi skirt, with a shirt on top. The beach had a large surf break near shore and the sand had been chiselled on a sharp angle down to the water. I was not a strong swimmer so didn't venture in, preferring to splash around in the shallows. It was really a great respite from travelling to be here and enjoy a hot climate by a beach. I was still very aware I was not in Australia though so I had to be cautious. There were no flags to swim between!

One day while sitting on the beach a young boy of about eight carrying a large hatchet in one hand and string of coconuts in the other walked slowly along and then stopped in front of me. He chopped the top off the coconut with three quick small chops and passed it over to me to drink. It was so delicious! I guzzled it and then slowed down to savour it. In the heat it was really refreshing. The boy sat down next to me while I slowly finished it off. This was my first of many coconut drinks, and at one rupee was a bargain.

While in Hikkaduwa I got to know some of the shopkeepers, and one guy who worked in a café, possibly a little younger than myself, offered to be my guide for a day. He took me to a special Buddhist monastery. He said there was a monk there who was from New Zealand originally and maybe I would like to see him. The only thing was that the monks had a vow of silence, so I would not be able to talk to him.

So, we chose a day and time that worked for him and the monastery. I was again reminded that some people thought that I was a Buddhist. I must have looked the part—my hair was quite short, I wore no make-up or jewellery, wore simple shirts and trousers in white, orange, and maroon, and I only had one small backpack. This assumption seemed more common now, as Sri Lanka's major religion was Buddhism.

We had to take a crowded but friendly local bus along past a few coastal towns with standing room only. When we got off I followed my guide along a well-trodden wide path through a fabulous lush tropical forest.

We then visited a large home owned by a wealthy family friend of his. He described it as a traditional Sri Lankan home. It had open dark wooden window shutters that allowed the breeze to flow through. There were large ceiling fans, a dining table, and other carved furniture all in the similar dark wood. It was well decorated with large vases, flowers, and plants.

We carried on walking until we reached a break in the forest and I saw the brackish waters of Ratgama Lake. On the other side of this small lake was an island with a temple and other buildings. In order to get there, we had to sit on log catamarans that would take two people each. So, I got on one behind a man who paddled slowly on either side of our log seat.

He warned me to keep my feet on the log and to not dangle them in the water. I saw why very soon as the lake was full of creatures that looked like an eel crossed with a lizard. He indicated that they might bite your feet. I pressed my feet very firmly to the log to make sure they didn't fall into the water, and that made him laugh.

This island temple was a simple structure on the outside but it was quite different on the inside. There was a large room for worship with monks sitting in rows. We were silent as we walked through. In the front shrine area, statues and walls were brightly coloured with glossy paint. It was called the Island Hermitage and was set up by a German who had become a fully ordained Buddhist monk in the early twentieth century. It also had an extensive library for study. I was not a Buddhist but if I was, I might have come back there again. I felt very welcome to.

We walked the corridors that surrounded the central temple accompanied by a couple of monks. One monk acted as a guide as he was allowed to speak to me a little in English. There I saw slightly larger than life-size statues of characters and scenery that told Buddhist stories. I'm not sure if I fully understood was he was saying but I think this display was the life of Buddha and epic stories, something like the Mahabharata. I noticed Krishna and some of the main deities. The statues were very lifelike and painted with a great degree of detail like hyper realistic portraits.

We were then shown around the paths on the island. There were several other buildings. There was a monk who we saw for a few moments walking steadily in the distance on a connecting smaller island, who then disappeared into the landscape. My guide told me that was the New Zealand monk. Apparently, they had told him an Australian was visiting today.

We travelled back to Hikkaduwa as the sun set. My habit was not to go out at night much, going to bed early and getting up early instead. I had dinner; my guide came back and was giving me compliments and kind of asking me out. He said he had an Italian girlfriend once. I simply declined as graciously as I could and it seemed to be fine, except the following day he ignored me. And this is why I didn't go out at night alone. I didn't want the attention and possible hassles. I had resigned myself to it. The same at home really.

On the 29th of August I was back in Colombo. I had a lot of time that day before I got on my flight back to India, so I decided to walk to the airport. When I only had about two miles to go I walked into a chicken hatchery shop to ask directions. There were dozens of baby birds under warming lights in glass boxes. The people in the shop were very interested in me and asked lots of questions.

The next thing I knew they had called their relatives and were taking me home for lunch. I had a meal with about twenty people. It was my send-off party from Sri Lanka. They said if *their* daughter were travelling, they would hope someone would also be friendly to her. It was great and they were lovely people. I saw their fully laden feijoa tree and said yes, I did like the fruit so they picked a bag of them for me to take. They gave me bags of tea and coffee and other small gifts to give my family, which I posted home. Then they all waved as I left.

As I arrived at the airport I saw Anna and Tim. I felt a small jolt inside, as it was a bit awkward. I waved from a distance to indicate that I was alive and well. I gave them their space, as that is what they had wanted. We might meet up later in Calcutta. I had also moved on within myself. I would have preferred company but I was actually okay on my own.

Tiruchirappalli, Madras, Pondicherry, Puri

BACK IN INDIA I visited the Srirangam, which was an island part of the city of Tiruchirappalli (called Trichy for short) in

Tamil Nadu. I did the tourist office day tour of the city to get my bearings. I could not wait to visit this island towering over the surrounding town. It had fortress walls, which enclosed a small ancient city including several amazing temples.

I meandered through this complex of buildings. Some looked older while others were being restored with new stonework. Stunning multi-coloured paint was the final step. There were seemingly infinite combinations of intricately carved plinths, columns, walls, and corridors. There were tall, impressive gate towers and several internal temple areas, which were mesmerizing. Two rivers passing on either side created this island Srirangam. So outside, there were also river views and city views.

On the 6th of September I was in Madras. This city was large and impressive with large formal colonial style buildings perhaps used for government or business. It reminded me of Sydney. I also spent a day visiting the local T.M. Centre there.

The T.M. Centre was a large colonial home with a meandering path through its large, shady, and colourful garden. I spoke with a T.M. teacher and then took a walk with him in the garden. I felt very welcomed. We talked about all their facilities there. He showed me other buildings that included two rows of individual studio accommodation on either side of a courtyard. People would come to stay and do meditation courses. The teacher said there was a course on at the moment so I couldn't look inside, as the rooms were full.

I was interested in doing some courses there, but he said I would have to go back and do them in Australia as English would not generally be spoken. I wasn't ready to go back. I still had time and money to go further. I would find a centre in Melbourne and find out more maybe next year.

Next was Pondicherry, a busy beach town settled by the French, with a rocky, windy, and rambling east coast facing the Bay of Bengal. I stayed at one of the Sri Aurobindo Ashram's guest houses there. I had heard from other travellers, that it was the most comfortable one and the income from the guest houses helped to fund the ashram. I had seen Aurobindo incense for sale in Melbourne so knew they had cottage industries too.

I arrived at the accommodation and was given several slips of paper: a map of the ashram's facilities, and vouchers for the morning yoga classes, the dining room, the library, and an orientation tour of the town and shops. All these were included in the accommodation cost. In one way I felt suddenly institutionalised but in another I just felt cared for. I felt very relaxed. I was quite confident with my independence and freedom now, but this community was a rest from constantly being alert for my safety. There were both many Indians and foreigners from many countries living there.

The meals were served in a huge old house. Hundreds of people would file through, collect a thali plate and be served vegetarian Indian food. After eating at long share tables we rinsed our plates and cutlery under a row of taps and left them for others to collect. The place operated like clockwork.

I went on a small group tour. We didn't see the whole of the town but just those facilities that were part of the ashram. There were various buildings that produced necessities such as food, clothing, incense, and soap, and there was a large bookshop. Going into one building I was amazed that inside its doors and courtyard gates was a fully working dairy. There were many cows grazing on feed, milking stalls, and milk processing rooms. Then the gates closed, and it seemed like a regular streetscape again.

The tour ended at the main ashram house where we were told the story of the ashram and its original teachers. There was an extensive fresh flower display at the central shrines of the Samadhi place of Sri Aurobindo and the Mother (Mirra Alfassa).

In the dining room I met Shanti, an elderly Indian man with snow-white hair. He was delightful and very interested in world philosophies, so we talked at length some days. He told me about

Sri Aurobindo the founder of the group who was a politician, philosopher, and poet before he started this ashram in the 1920s. The main precepts were based on doing regular yoga and meditation, eating well, and caring for yourself and others.

Shanti would take me to the yoga classes, which he had been doing for many years. I think he enjoyed meeting travellers to hear about other places. We often ate together too. I felt sad to leave him as I travelled on. He was such a sweet man. He reminded me of my Dad.

I visited Puri and some temples there, such as the Shree Jagannath Temple. They had a distinct architecture style. Their towers were beehive shaped and decoration was more organic rather than human figure carvings. There were remnants of an old temple on the beach that the water had reclaimed, with parts of statues in the sand.

Shree Jagannath Temple, Puri.

I also went to a very expansive marketplace in Puri. The stalls were not jammed up close together and there was space for children to play and groups of young boys playing cricket. More than once I joined in and even had a bat. I had done this in a few other towns as well over the last few months. I was not very good, but it was always fun or at least I provided some amusement. I would not have done this at the start of my trip but felt way more confident now.

When it came to cricket everyone spoke English, knew the names of teams and players, the score of important matches going on, and often would have a transistor radio to let me hear the scores. When I said I was Australian that was always a draw card to get a bat. I think they thought I might be good. Occasionally I did hit a big one. My youngest sister and my older brother had both played competitive cricket and we often played in our back yard. So, I had the idea.

I also really wanted to eat a samosa, as they smelt so good, but when I looked at them I saw they were stacked in a pyramid, with a small swarm of flies over them. What to do? Before cooking, the samosas were covered. I watched the process and saw that the last step was a ferociously hot deep-fry in oil in a large wok. The cook then scooped them out one at a time with a draining spoon and added them to the stack. So, I grabbed a paper bag, pointed into the wok and got a fresh hot one straight from the spoon. It was delicious.

At this market I decided to do something that I normally didn't do. I decided to take photos of people. I would try to ask their permission before I did it and if they declined I would leave them alone. Usually I felt shy or vulnerable in some way or sometimes it felt invasive. I had a very small and quite amateurish camera.

It seemed to be going okay, with a few *yes* and *no* reactions. Then I saw a commanding Saddhu with long dreadlocks tied up in a pile on his head. As I indicated I'd like to take a photo he said nothing. I looked through the lens to show him the idea and he looked back at me with a strong stare. I was confused but he stood as if posing so I took what was an amazing portrait. I thanked him and left. When I got back to my hotel room, I found that the film had not rolled onto its spool properly. I hadn't got any images at all! I never really tried to take portraits like that again.

How to Get on a Bus

THERE WERE OTHER events that were in one sense quite mundane but also a challenge. In one town (the name of which wasn't noted in my diary) I had stayed overnight in a simple one-room wooden bungalow. Across the road was a large bus depot. There was a couple of acres of concrete dotted with a few concrete bus shelters and stops. So, it was a bleak landscape.

During the night someone tried to open my door but I had it padlocked from the inside, so they just went away. As they did not try in earnest and I heard them try other doors nearby I figured the person might have just been looking for somewhere to sleep. I tried not to panic. After a while, I made myself go back to sleep.

The next morning I could not believe I had handled that scary incident so nonchalantly. I guess I had no choice. I was just being reminded again of my vulnerability as I was on my own. I couldn't dwell on it too long as it would kill my confidence. I got up and got ready to go.

There was not much decoration, landscaping, or shops around the bus depot, so it seemed visually to my mind like a stage where characters came and went. No one seemed to speak English. I thought it would be easy to wander over in the morning, work out my connection and hop on a bus. This was not so.

I had worked out my stop and then waited relaxedly as there were hardly any people around. There wasn't even a formal queue there. I carried cash for the ticket and the rest of the day in my top pocket and had water and food ready for the journey.

As the bus slowly dawdled its way into the station and then over to my stop, out of nowhere came lots of other passengers. They knew precisely when to turn up and an intense crush of people swarmed at the bus door. I tried to get on the bus but as people pushed on and off through the single door, the bus filled as if magically before my eyes. Some other passengers and I didn't get on. I wasn't willing to sit on the roof, if indeed I could have climbed up there, as some young guys did.

Okay, so what to do? The next time I knew the spot to stand and I would be at the front. I checked with others for the next bus time and thought again I was ready. A few other buses came and went at different spots in the concrete square. About an hour later another bus pulled in slowly, steadily, and came to rest near my stop again, but a short distance from where it had been last time. I was again not at the front of the crush of people who magically arrived and swarmed to get on board. I tried a little more earnestly but again did not end up on the bus and it left again. I was now getting just a little desperate.

So, the third time an hour later again when my bus ambled over to somewhere near my pick-up stop, I stood back and thought about my plan of attack. And I was thrown a lifeline. I saw three European tourists on that bus and they spoke English. They worked their way over to the window I was looking in. The windows didn't have glass but were just open spaces with metal bars across the space.

I only had a small bag, so I pushed it in between the bars and asked them to hold me a seat until I got on. Of course, this was a gamble, but I had to take it and they spread out to keep the space using my bag as a prop. Again, what choice did I have? I had all my essentials on me: money, cheques, passport etc. The bag had clothes, toiletries and books.

I threw myself into the crush this time because my bag was on board! No more polite, physical space between people. I was calling out to my new friends on board and they called out back to me, so the other people kind of let me on, thinking I was joining them. So, it worked.

We said our fond farewells, even though we had just met! They left the bus and I was left wondering why I was still travelling on my own. How could I find others to travel with? Could I have gone with those people? Should I go home? I had no answers at the moment.

I realised there was a women's section on the bus, so I wiggled my way between everyone indicating I was heading over there and found myself a very tight but welcome seat in the middle of a row of women. One elderly woman was wailing at me as she thought I was a man. Luckily her daughter reassured her I was female and then turned to me and told me in English it was okay. I sat next to her happily.

Bus Stop

THIS BUS TRIP was an all-day venture. I was wedged in a seat in the ladies' section of three rows towards the back with my small pack on my lap. I could lean forward and doze on it and get the water bottle for sipping. The bus stopped at many small villages and slightly larger towns.

Each time we stopped there was movement on and off the bus that was slow and intense, as there never seemed to be enough seats for everyone wanting to get on. There were sudden surges of pushing at times and then slower often verbally directed negotiations between people. I was pleased that I didn't have to get off at any of those stops. I felt that I would never get back on.

I had been sipping water for a long time. My bladder had to handle it as there was no way I would be able to visit a toilet at a bus stop and get back on the bus. On other bus trips toilets were also not very clean due to the large numbers of people visiting the stations. I hung on and hung on for hours, distracting myself by sleeping, meditating, looking out this window and then that window.

Then I started getting desperate. At one point I just stood up. The bus was moving along a wide and long straight stretch of road. I wasn't sure what my plan was, but I couldn't hold on any longer. So, I excused myself to all the ladies I squeezed past in my row. There was an aisle at one side of the bus. When I got there, I worked my way between the crush of standing men saying, "Excuse me" and "Thanks" as I went. Occasionally I thought maybe someone spoke English as they replied but mostly they just stared at me. We were nowhere near a bus stop so why was I moving to the front of the bus as if to get off? The whole busload of people was watching me inch to towards the driver.

I made it to him but he didn't speak English. So, I put my pack down right next to him on the floor. I pointed to my stomach region rather than my private parts and then pointed to the door. He got it immediately and slammed on the brakes. He then pulled the bus over to one side of the road and opened the door for me. He was smiling, and I was smiling. I thought we were communicating fine. So, I looked back at my bag and indicated that I'd be back for it. What could possibly go wrong?

As I got off the bus everyone's eyes were following me. I was going to head for the nearby forest. But then I heard it. He was driving off, slowly at first and then faster. I did panic a little. But I really needed to relieve myself above all else! I looked up and tried to engage with the driver again but could not see his face. I took a deep breath. I would have to chase the bus after I had a pee.

There were some huge cement pipes sitting on top of the soil along the road's edge waiting to be laid. I made a beeline for them, so I could finally relieve myself behind them. As I reached the pipes the bus stopped, about two hundred metres away. He had moved the bus along to give me some privacy.

After I was finished I jogged to the bus, got on, thanked him in English and various words in Hindi. I picked up my bag and worked my way back into the rear women's rows. I was proud that it had all worked out. I sat there and relaxed. Then I realised in the rush of the moment I had not fully emptied my bladder and I still had a small sense that I needed to go again. I had to hang on again for the last hour or so.

Heaven in a Field

DURING ANOTHER LONG trip the bus stopped and everyone got off but we were not yet at our destination. I was not aware that I needed to change buses when I had got on. The driver and passengers assured me in mostly non-English words that I had to get off here too. They gestured, and I understood that I should follow them, as there would be another bus to finish our journey. So off we went walking through a small village. We turned a corner and went over the crest of a small hill.

As I looked up it seemed that I was walking into heaven. Surrounding me was a picture perfect postcard scene set on an almost flat but very gradual convex hilltop. The sky was a soft baby blue with immaculate, fluffy, cumulus clouds slowly drifting across it. The sunlight was mellow and warm. The breeze was refreshing as it massaged my face. The air was crisp and clean as it entered my lungs. There were fields of crops of varying colours and heights dotted with the occasional leafy or flowering trees. Some of these trees had groups of workers sitting under them. Perhaps it was lunch break. They were chatting, laughing, and some were dozing. Time had slowed down for me.

While my feet and body walked at a steady and brisk pace to keep up with the group of people I was with, my eyes wandered slowly all over this scene, soaking it in. Perhaps I had been in towns too long and the country was such a delight on this beautiful day. I breathed in the variety of smells from my sweat to the crops and blossoms. I didn't really know what many of these plants were.

As we trotted along on a path through a field and then back onto a semi-main perimeter road of compressed and slightly dusty mud, I had to come to a stop. A very tall woman in a sari stood in my way. I wasn't sure what was going on. She held a large basket on her head with one hand. She held up her other hand in front of me to stop me.

Then she lowered the basket down off her head. It had been sitting on a small bundle of cloth, which acted as a cushion. The contents of the basket were a surprise. It held another bundle of fabric and a slightly dented brass teapot, which I presumed to be full of chai, and many terracotta chai cups.

She sat the basket on the ground in front of me to ensure that I wouldn't stray. She gently unpacked the cloth bundle, pulled out one large warm chapatti and gave it to me. While I took a large bite she poured me a cup of chai in a small terracotta cup. I was used to this kind of tea and loved it. We watched each other, eye to eye and became instant friends. I missed my friends and family but I found support in meeting wonderful people like her along the way. I craved human connection at times. The chapatti was not only satisfying but made me realise how hungry I was.

The woman was now smiling broadly. She was so kind; she kept her eye on the line of bus passengers and assured me with her raised hand that I had time to finish her meal. There was no rush. It was true the line of people I was walking with had now spread out and there were still many behind me. Her job was to feed the field workers, but she had chosen to feed me too. I felt really nurtured by this exchange.

It was a shame I had to go on. I would gladly have stayed longer with her and helped her give out chapattis and tea. She packed everything back into her basket and put it back on her head. We bowed to each other and reluctantly split up.

I walked on again gaining speed to keep up with my fellow bus passengers and she walked into the field nearby, towards a tree with workers under it. We both looked back at each other. I took in a last glance of that delightful scenery and then descended down a path towards our next bus.

Monkeys on a Train

ON ONE TRIP I was on a train that had no glass in the windows, just metal bars across the window openings. I had been warned that as we pulled into the next station the train would be inundated with monkeys who would move through the train with light fingers. Apparently, they would steal food, or anything not pinned down. It was a major station, so we would stay there for some time as many passengers would get off and the train would fill up with new ones.

I watched the other passengers prepare for the onslaught. They put away glasses in bags so I did too. They took off all jewellery and locked it away. I was wearing none. The same with watches, pens, or anything else in shirt or suit pockets, loose items, but rings stayed on. So, I copied them and checked with them that I had done enough.

I felt quite confident, as they had all survived the event before, right? They told me to cover my eyes and roll up in a ball with my face buried into my backpack to cover any pockets in the pack that may be opened by nimble fingers.

Then it began. As we slowly glided into our simple cement platform, which was one of many in a row, I could see *flocks* of monkeys sprinting towards our train. It should be troops of monkeys but they weren't in any way an orderly group. They split up into battalions and dove at the various carriages. They appeared to be flying as they reached the windows.

They were screeching as if to add drama and menace, and to increase fear, which did really work. Luckily this experience was not at the very beginning of my trip or I might have gone straight home. They flew in the window to my left; I was second from the window. They would for a moment cuddle and run their hands over one passenger and then the next. Just in case they had missed anything the next monkey did the same.

I did not look up but experienced it all by touch, hearing, and smell. I felt my sweaty body tense up. I felt their active, agile bodies. They would fly in and crash into you, scurrying to get vertical again and lightly pick at you. I intermittently heard children screaming, women screaming, and angry words from others. I smelt monkey skin and the sweat and perfumes of humans. I smelt the distant smell of chai and puris cooking.

My head was tucked down into my bag but my peripheral vision saw intense eyes, bottoms, hands, and talon-like nails on monkey fingers, and other nearby huddled passengers. My mind was reeling. *Have I been vaccinated for this? They moved fast. How many were there?* Then they were gone.

They were moving through the train so rapidly I had no time to be frightened out of my skin. In two or three minutes it was over. Others showed me to look out the windows on the far side of the carriage and these *troops* were flying off into the distance as they had come. They said the monkeys didn't stay long or the station staff would get them.

The Bikers

AFTER ANOTHER LONG train trip, I got off and walked over to sit on the bench seat in the middle of the platform to collect myself. I was looking around as everyone unloaded onto the platform. It was a busy scene with lots of people moving around, carrying luggage, boxes, and merchandise and calling out instructions to each other. The bench where I was sitting quickly filled up with other alighting passengers doing the same. We nodded and smiled at each other. No one had yet spoken English but I knew a few Hindi words so could follow a little of what was going on around me.

Suddenly I found myself watching what looked like a clip from the movie *Easy Rider*. It had two larger-than-life characters. The spectacle began. Out from the next carriage stepped a tallish non-Indian traveller with his girlfriend. They both wore tight pants or jeans, white billowing long sleeve shirts and leather jackets. They both had long hair that blew out behind them as if there was a wind machine. His hair was a lighter brown than hers, almost blond. I thought they might be European but then through the melee of people my eyes locked onto his and we nodded. He was Australian for sure.

They were clearly very conscious that everyone was now looking at them. He strode to a further away train compartment and then walked back confidently rolling a huge motorbike with high handlebars. Then the crowds came. The few of us sitting on the bench had to sit up to see more clearly as the biker and his girlfriend were now surrounded by dozens of people watching silently in a kind of awe. I tried to be nonchalant but was enjoying this unusual yet also mundane event.

While she fixed her hair and held on to their luggage, he began strapping on their bags and a guitar to the metal rack at the back of the bike. He then tied large shiny glinting heavy metal chains around and around the luggage and locked them, perhaps with a padlock but I couldn't see this clearly through the crowds.

Then he gave a smiling sweeping glance around the crowd and gripped the handlebars while he swung his leg over into the driver's seat. She balanced herself on his arm and swung herself into her seat close behind him. He switched on the bike with a roar. Some of the crowd leant in while others leant out. Those in front realised they had to move out of the way as the bikers wanted to drive forward. I felt as if I was watching TV and the show was a parody of cool bikers.

The driver revved the motor a few times and walked the bike forward a little as if indicating that he needed a clear path to drive off. And then they did. With a series of large revs the bike drove slowly and then gained momentum as the path opened up. They roared off the end of the platform and into the distance leaving behind a trail of smoke and noise.

Night Trains

ON ONE NIGHT train I had booked the top bunk, which was a wooden slat bench that pulled down from the wall, transforming the day carriage into a sleeper carriage.

Earlier while we were all still seated in the compartment, I chatted with a father of six daughters, of whom he was very proud. Every year he went around India by train to visit temples dedicated to the female deities. This was his devotion to his family with whom he was "Blessed".

He was surprised, if not a little shocked and anxious, that as a twenty-two-year-old female I was travelling on my own. I explained that it was not by choice but it was my gap year and my friends had stopped travelling. What was I to do, be brave or go home? I also had no idea how to find new travelling companions. So he asked many questions as you do of a stranger.

Then he advised me in a very parental way, with a cautious hug, to not forget to keep time to have relationships, so as to experience the full range of life rather than always being on my own.

On my bunk bed I used my pack as my pillow with one lungi sheet underneath and another on top of me. I had bought these two lungis at a market somewhere along the way. Wherever I stayed I laid one on top of the bed and over the pillow, and used one as the top sheet. I washed them often and this afforded me the comfort of not worrying too much about the mattress or bedding in any backpacker accommodation. The bed was quite high and so was pretty close to the ceiling but it felt very private and secure up there and I slept well.

Bananas

One afternoon on a bus I was on my own and I decided I was ready to do some bartering. I noticed that at markets I had been getting considerably less bananas per rupee than the locals. I was in luck as I leaned out the window of my bus. There were three banana sellers in a row competing for my business. So I played them off against each other.

When I got to ten bananas per rupee they all started showing the pain so I knew they were about at their limit. The final bid was eleven bananas for one rupee and I took the deal. They were the smaller Lady Finger type. Clearly I didn't really need eleven but they were always good to have when travelling, I could share them and they would keep.

As the bus took off and I looked back at my banana sellers they were clearly giving more than eleven to a woman so I hadn't really got my bargain. They probably had been acting and working me, as a team.

PART 3

Calcutta to Nepal, Trekking, Some Northern Indian Cities, and Bangkok to Melbourne

Calcutta Again

I ARRIVED BACK in Calcutta on the 13th of September at 8:20 a.m. on a train from Puri. I hailed a taxi but the driver wanted to take an extra person. I didn't feel comfortable about that so after a short yelling match he decided that transporting only me would be okay. His mood switched immediately back to being super polite. We drove off across a bridge and merged into the pathos and swarming traffic of the morning rush hour.

It felt like I was beginning a different phase in my travel. Calcutta seemed strange, as it was both familiar yet new at the same time. I did know where I wanted to go and how to get there which was helpful. There were familiarities all around me but I had seen so much and changed a lot since last here. I looked forward to exploring more in Calcutta, planning my next few weeks in Nepal, and feeling less caught up with anxiety. I was enjoying this moment.

Today I also received a letter at the Poste Restante office from Anna, Tim, and another person Lucy, who would meet up with me here in a few days. I booked us two double rooms at the Red Shield Guest House so I would share with Lucy and we could also buy breakfast there.

When they arrived it was strangely natural and we picked up with no awkwardness from splitting up. Then we set off around Calcutta. They had decided to also come to Nepal. They would spend one week in Nepal whereas I would stay longer, for at least a month.

We took a taxi to the post office where I picked up some more letters. There was one from Ryan, who was now leaving Srinagar. I had missed him at times but thought how bored I would have been staying there all this time. I felt stimulated and stronger from my travels. I felt he had missed out.

I was not yet finished with India and still had a few other places I wanted to visit, such as Varanasi and Rishikesh. These ancient spiritual places held a romantic mystique for me.

There was a letter from Mum with news about the family and that she had transferred some money from my account in Melbourne to the State Bank of India in Calcutta to make sure I didn't run out. I read her letter quickly but always re-read them many times when I needed some company. Everyone was okay. My youngest sister had got engaged.

We passed through a crooked intersection, and then right at the far end of Sudder Street. We were looking for a meal. We got out of our taxi and checked out the Fairview Hotel but the meals were only for the residents. We then went around to the YMCA. Today it was darker inside, crowded. We sipped drinks sitting on metal chairs on the balcony. It was spitting rain so many people had gone inside. I had a chai and several samosas, one rupee each. After a while we went back down Sudder St. to the Oasis Restaurant. The weather was still quite hot. We had only drunk a lot of Limcas today while walking around so it was good to have some solid food there.

We went home to read, wash clothes, and sleep. After walking all day, I had a much better sleep than the previous night.

The next day was Friday. I went downstairs and put my packed bag in a locker, shared a taxi with the other three and they dropped me off at the bank to collect my six hundred dollar transfer. I was so used to looking after myself now that I didn't feel too caught up in what the others wanted to do. I couldn't collect the transfer because the banks were not open due to a strike.

The sun had been soft this morning but gradually was becoming stronger. It was good walking around now early before the heat and crowds. I went on to the British Airways office to enquire about possible future flights. I asked about changing money and they reassured me the moneychangers at New

Market would be working today and they were safe enough. I wanted to change some Indian rupees to Nepalese, as that is where we were headed now. I remembered where it was so headed off walking again along past chanting groups of bank strikers with red banners.

I felt pretty relaxed despite this run-around, not paranoid, just acting and not overthinking much. Maybe it was the heat. Maybe I was stunned by what I had to do. I was swinging my umbrella as I walked through an archway and shaking off the hawkers.

I was not interested in anything much at the market and could only see plastic shopping baskets, saris, and kids' t-shirts. I felt nostalgic when remembering I had shopped here with Ryan and Adrian earlier. I felt a lot less anxious now.

I cut up the back then to the side exit and left up Sudder St. and to see Mr. Kapoor at the AUS Office. I really enjoyed his company. He sort of remembered me and asked where my two friends were now. There was a girl reading a brown paper covered novel who was watching me write down my plans for future travel options. I looked down and my feet were really dirty.

Mr. Kapoor advised me a lot. He gave me information about flights and would send me a letter to Kathmandu with more details. He also advised me to write from Kathmandu to the State Bank in Calcutta to ask them to hold my money, and ask them to write back to me to confirm that this was okay.

I walked back to the Red Shield Guest House and then to check out the Woodlands Vegetarian Restaurant. There was a nice waiter who saw me outside, invited me in, and struck up a conversation. "Where were you from in Australia?" It was good there, and cool. There were four people, Aussies maybe, listening to a Pommy cricket commentator. It reminded me of home a little, but not enough to want to talk to them while I ate.

Afterwards I checked out the Oberoi Grand Hotel, which had posh, white garden furniture around the pool in the outside courtyard. I had some afternoon tea there. I felt good walking around Calcutta afterwards and felt just a little speedy from the strong tea.

I went back to the Red Shield and was sitting in the lounge when Anna, Tim and Lucy arrived. They had been shopping. They had many shirts and skirts. Lucy showed off an embroidered sari petticoat, which she could wear as a skirt when not in India. I spluttered out the story of my day, showing my market purchases of fruit and shampoo. I was enjoying being with them, having companions to go with to Nepal but also I was very much okay on my own now.

Headed North

SO WE HEADED off in a taxi. This morning the sun had been low on the horizon yet really bright and blinding. Now as we drove passed trees and buildings the even stronger afternoon light was flickering with so much visual chaos that I had to keep my head down.

As we got our luggage out of the car boot at Howrah Station a scene caught my attention. There was a man who looked like he was a Yogi or Baba with a long grey beard, Ghandi topi (or Gujarati white cap), and floral garlands around his neck. He sat cross-legged with a group of young and old men around him. They all sat very still and silent. By contrast, the voice of beggars seated nearby was demanding attention in my left ear.

It now felt like it was the beginning of *another* new phase in my travelling. I was daydreaming about things I had seen lately, such as, people sleeping, even living in the train stations and streets. We entered this station through a tall metal turnstile gate at the entrance of a high chain-link fence and walked up a sloping, concrete ramp bordered by strong metal bars. Two men behind this fence looked into my eyes, held up their two hands pressed together as a blessing and nodded.

Just as I found our carriage and seats numbers listed near one carriage door, a Sikh man stepped back kindly and let us go in onto the train. Once inside there were two other Sikhs wanting the same sleeper seat and arguing politely. Then I saw a relaxed colourfully clothed arm hanging on to the rail near one compartment. I hoped it was the ladies' compartment. It was and this girl's seat was opposite mine. Her sari had a blue and gold paisley border on a white background. Anna, Lucy, and I were able to get sleeper seats, and paid for them on the train. Added to our ticket price was a one hundred rupees departure from India tax.

The taxi driver we just used charged only three rupees to Howrah Station and quoted twenty-five to Dum Dum Airport. I would look for him next time in Calcutta, as these were good rates. I had learnt about fair prices by now. He had transfers stuck on his windscreen with the busts of what I thought were Sikh gods but it turned out that these were the ten earthly manifestations, ten gurus and not gods. There was only one God in Sikhism. He talked about the question of the last Sikh God, which I didn't understand. Maybe he was talking about the last Guru rather than the last God.

There were also some Dutch travellers on our train. They looked as if they were high and tripping. They were concerned that they were running out of tablets to give their friends for diarrhoea and were asking around for more. I thought they were dangerous and unpredictable to be with and luckily didn't really give us much attention at all.

There was also that sentimental group of men from outside the station seeing their Baba or Guru off on to the train. I looked on and thought, *What do we know?*

I had been travelling for months and I still gazed wistfully out the train windows, this time at the sun behind the palm trees. I watched the country go by as we were leaving India and heading to Nepal.

Nepal

THE TRAIN LEFT Howrah Station at 4:25 that afternoon and would arrive at 7:00 a.m. the next morning at Muzzaffarpur. Then there would be a three-hour bus to Raxaul, for thirty-two rupees. We had sleepers and Tim was next door with three Germans. It was such nice tropical country with small local train platforms to look at intermittently. I had a window seat.

There were a lot of green water ponds and overgrown land around the stations, and small mud brick and brick houses along the tracks. Children walked and ran next to the train. There was a cement bridge then acres of rice paddies and then overgrown lush verdant backyards backing on to the train line. I saw a large umbrella hanging up in a backyard. There were feathery looking plants growing in lush fields with short brick fences.

I liked the chai on the train, and also watched the coffee sellers, but the cups were so small I thought they were mean. It was very hot and I had sweat running down my back, armpits, and legs inside my clothes. I saw one large palm with a very fluffy top in the centre. I was writing instead of watching. The observer was the observed.

In the bush the train passed a brick building with a large green and white sign, which read *Vivekananda Ashram*. I was eating bananas and oranges. There was a sunset; yellow behind the clouds then an intense orange as the light was coming out of grey clouds again. There was a pink haze on the grey as well. Anna tried to photograph the sublime scene before it disappeared behind the carriages in a rail yard. Then the pink sky under the grey had a red disc peeking out at the top, through dark green trees and light rain. There were many large water buffalos in the farmyards abutting the train line.

People were saying "Acha" again, which could mean anything from *yeah*, to *nice*, to *all right* or *whatever*. We all seemed happy, talking and helping each other. We were sitting up on our wooden bench beds watching the electricity storm while sweating dirt inside our clothes in the heat.

I got to know two nearby Sikhs who had no covers or bags. They shared a dinner and simply lay down and slept. One took his turban off which Lucy described as "yards and yards" of fabric. There were small boys in khaki shorts, selling salted breads in rolled up newspaper at the station. I was thinking of going home again and had just written to three friends from art school.

I slept on the bottom bunk, where there was a lot of soot, and I found a pen refill on the floor. I would try it to see if it fitted my pens. After a brekkie cup of chai, while watching mesmerized as the Sikhs wound their turbans back on, I did a couple of short meditations. Then abruptly we were off the train.

We caught rickshaws to the Raxaul bus depot, for one rupee each. It was muddy, the streets were quite rundown, and there were old broken-down buses lining the road. There seemed to be no real depot but lots of people. A random man was fighting some rickshaw men there. We were working through the difficult bits of travelling to get to the good bits. We could have flown but wanted to go at least one way on the ground to check it out.

Our bus turned out to be a minibus. We paid ten rupees each and then we had to really squash up. Along with me, Lucy, Anna and Tim, there were two Tibetan soldiers, a thin Indian with an extremely smooth face, and several others.

I was trying to lighten the mood by talking about cricket and also starting a conversation about comparing Kathmandu and Nepal with Switzerland.

We had a stop for chai that cost forty-five paisa and some arrowroot biscuits in a really dirty wrapper for one rupee.

It began spitting with rain then gradually there was so much rain that the packs on the roof of the minibus were soaked through. So people covered their packs with clothes in lieu of a tarpaulin. It ended up that we would only pay six and a half rupees to the bus depot across the border as we all complained on being squashed in.

Our passports were stamped as we arrived at Birgunj on the 15th of September 1979. I noted this mentally too as my Nepal Visa was for thirty days, issued on the 13th of September 1979 by the Consulate General in Calcutta. I was thinking about what I could fit in during that time.

Just as we arrived and were unloading in Birgunj a nearby trishaw overturned in the mud, snagged and tore my maroon trousers. This was a real drag, as I liked these ones while my other trousers were more functional than desirable.

We went to the Diyalo Hotel that we saw opposite the bus rank. It was forty-five rupees per double room (1 Indian Rupee to one forty-five Nepalese). For late lunch we were really hungry and had veg paratha, veg soup, veg fried rice, soda, and tea, which was thirteen rupees. We emptied out our wet clothes from our bags. We sat out on the roof lounge for a while.

It felt a bit strange that all the people hanging out in the hotel instead of being Indian were now Chinese. I slept and was dead to the world when Anna, Tim, and Lucy blew some kind of horn for dinner. I was a bit disorientated but got up, as I was really hungry again.

I think I had a fever coming. I hoped it was just a cold and nothing more serious. I wondered where I might find a doctor.

After dinner I did some washing and then went to sleep early. I slept lightly under no cover that night.

I woke up at 5:30 a.m. the next day for our twelve-hour bus trip to Kathmandu. I had a fever but it was manageable. I started folding things, and got down to a brekkie of tea, toast, and cornflakes. When we got to the bus stand in time to catch the 7:00 a.m. bus we found it had left ten minutes ago. We had not changed our watches and Nepal time was fifteen minutes ahead of Calcutta time. So we hopped in rickshaws and raced through the early morning town and beat the bus to the next stop.

This bus ride was magnificent. There were green rolling mountain ranges in the foreground, and seemingly infinite blue ranges in the distance. There were terraced corn crops and a deeply plunging valley. I was sketching. It was impossible to capture this but I enjoyed making lines, which was becoming very free due to lack of time to be precious.

We stopped for a break at a teahouse. There was a path up to a temple which I took as directed to find a place to pee. I saw a hill with a single small house on it with a brilliant white cloud dramatically behind it.

We drove on a bridge over a river. All sides of the land around us were built up and very green. I had a headache, had a cold coming on, and a sore throat. We arrived in Kathmandu and almost immediately a Chinese-looking man called out, "Two rickshaws?" We got in and away we swept up a wide avenue.

Kathmandu

THE KATHMANDU GUEST House where we had planned to stay was full. Nearby the Star Hotel was fine and I took a twin room with Lucy again for twenty rupees. She was easy to get along with but somehow I knew we might not meet again after the trip. So it's a very casual kind of friendship. We were thrown together but we looked out for each other and I enjoyed her happy company. We went next door to K.G.H. Restaurant before the rush came. The lights went off halfway through the meal so we had a candlelight dinner.

We went back upstairs. Lucy, Anna, and Tim wanted to go looking around shops so I stayed back, meditated, and rested up a bit. They all had much bigger backpacks and hand luggage than I had so they shopped for presents and clothes. That night none of us slept much or very well.

On Sunday my headache was still hanging on. The others hired bikes and I took a rickshaw to the post office. My rickshaw driver burst off at a really quick pace, and Tim tried riding in its slipstream but couldn't keep up and dropped back to the girls.

I had to wait for the post office to open at 10:00 a.m. There was a mountain man with a big beard, beggars, and kids with sores on their knees playing. I tickled one of the kids in his hand and make them all laugh. I finally got into the post office and found out that if there were letters, they were in alphabetical boxes that we could look through ourselves. Yes! I had a few letters from Mum, a sister, a school friend, and two very sweet friends from art school. One friend had become pregnant but lost the child. I felt sad for her. I kept reading and re-reading their letters. It was so good to have them all.

Then I walked down to various offices around the New Road area to orient myself and begin to research various trekking options including the Tourist Info Office and AUS Office. I made an appointment and came back later to see the trekking man.

I was wandering around the side streets and found MOM's Health Foods, where I had lunch with an Australian guy who was flying home via Perth. That was a shame, as he seemed like he would have been great company. I was still keeping my eye out for people to travel with. He was keen to get home and so then there was nothing much to talk about. I had never been to Perth but here I was in Nepal.

I got some good information about travel at the AUS Office. There were no special rates or charter flights for students. Most flights back to India were daily but I'd needed to give them five day's notice at least. To fly from Kathmandu to Patna was twenty dollars, then I could train Patna to Varanasi, then fly to Delhi, for about forty dollars, or fly directly Kathmandu to Delhi for seventy-four dollars.

One thing I noticed in both Kathmandu, and later Pokhara, was that there were an amazing number of coffee and cake shops, which I thought was great. They were mixed in with the variety of older shops. There were butchers with no fridges that hung the meat up from the ceiling and in the window in rows. There were dressmakers, knitted clothing stores, cafes, grocery and home ware shops and these cake shop cafes.

After months of Indian food I was able to eat a large slice of lemon meringue pie for lunch or black forest cake, carrot cake, chocolate cake, or cheesecake. Clearly I didn't order them all at once but there was great choice, served in generous slices large enough for a meal. At some point I realised these cake shops were really there servicing the dope smoking hippie trail travellers who had the munchies.

Bhaktapur

I WALKED EVERYWHERE in Kathmandu but would catch the local bus over to Bhaktapur, an extremely well-preserved medieval city less than an hour away. There were temples, palace buildings, and many were in and around the central Durbar Square. One day there were rows of large round clay pots drying in the sun. I never tired of the view of the mountains that surrounded all viewpoints in this town.

Pots drying in the sun.

As I left Bhaktapur one time a local public minibus pulled over that was full of Buddhist monks. I waved them on, as I didn't want to crowd them. They all laughed and called out at me, insisting I get in. They all squashed up and I squashed in. That was a very sweet and friendly ride. Maybe they thought I was a Buddhist too?

Back in Kathmandu I walked to the Tourist Info Office, and then to the big buildings of the Main Durbar Square and bazaar. I bought a cotton jumpsuit for my niece for forty rupees. I wondered how the family were. Things like this jumpsuit would trigger thoughts about home. People were sitting and sleeping around the ledges outside the very old temples and buildings in the square.

In the back streets there were not so many people. People were washing in pools that were down steps away from the square. The water came out from a carved dragon's mouth spout. Many babies were running around. Their mothers with groups of older kids were sitting by the water pump along with dogs and pigs.

I walked back up through side streets. There were several multi-storey houses in blocks, towering mountains behind them, snow on the mountain tops, and green open spaces. Most shops were pretty quiet. The streets were quite empty except for the occasional annoyance of a car driving through.

I was window-shopping. In one square, I found button through jackets with pockets for forty rupees, many rugs made from soft yak wool for six hundred rupees, and striped cotton shirts for twenty rupees. I really liked the throw rugs. I was enjoying seeing what was for sale in each place. I didn't buy much as it was too hard to carry more and I was budgeting.

I headed back home to rest and check on Lucy, who hadn't been feeling well. She was middling. She felt like eating which was a good sign. I wrote the names and addresses on all the aerograms and postcards I had bought with a green biro. I was clearing out my pack to keep it small. I emptied it out and made a packet of unnecessary things to gift on or throw out. Accumulations were amazing. Then I went into town to check out about going to Pokhara.

Last night the bats were screeching and laughing. Also last night as Lucy and I walked past a bike it suddenly jumped up and fell down noisily as if it was alive or possessed. We thought it was pretty funny.

We had dinner at Yes Yes Café then went back to the hotel to pay our bill and pack our gear. I wrapped extra junk into one lungi to store in the locked room downstairs. I could collect it when back in Kathmandu.

I was beginning to read *Lectures and Addresses* by Tagore. It was excellent to be reading philosophy again. I read that: my drawback was education as it encourages security and materialism, and it can also make you worry about time.

To Pokhara

ON WEDNESDAY THE 19th of September I was up at 5:30 a.m. We went down to get rickshaws. There was not much traffic but there were joggers. My pack was lighter so I was very happy about that. A light pack!

We arrived at the stop and climbed into a blue minibus that would take us to Pokhara. The trip would take most of the day. I sat three rows back from the front next to a civil engineer and a young Nepalese guy. We talked a lot about our own countries, imports and exports, populations, politics, dirty business, and losing contact with people over the years. I have increasingly enjoyed talking with strangers on this trip.

We stopped at chai shops. Outside one chai shop a woman was sewing and had several metres of grain spread out drying on the roadside, which was covered with dust. She had to guard the grain as there were many bright coloured chooks meandering and running around the street.

The bus continued on this way, driving and stopping at chai stops. It picked up extra passengers. If you wanted anything you banged on the bus wall, inside or out. The German girl opposite me was ill and needed a break at one point. There was another guy behind her who had a really nice smile, blonde flock of hair and a brilliant blue top. On my right side across the aisle was a man with extremely bony hands. He had a red and a yellow thread around his wrist and a prominent ring with a large jewel that shone with shards of red and yellow light.

We got in about 2 p.m. after about seven hours on the bus. We took a taxi to the lakeside. I saw glimpses of the peaks through the clouds. When the clouds dispersed later I saw the awesome immense circle of snow-covered mountains surrounding Pokhara.

Whenever the cloud cover disappeared the ring of mountains was so beautiful. I loved being in Pokhara with the mountains around all the time. It was breathtaking and they felt close. The power of nature and beauty was ever-present and sublime.

I walked to the Sherpa Trekking Co. office and got the prices to hire equipment and talked about hiring one Sherpa to take me trekking, carry my pack, and make sure I didn't get lost. They thought it was strange that I was on my own. What choice did I have? It was about sixty rupees per day.

I would have to fly back to Kathmandu to get my visa extended and stamped for trekking. To make arrangements they just needed one day's notice. So I would have to come back when I was ready to go. I walked down to the airways and booked the mid-morning Friday flight to Kathmandu.

I took some photos of water buffalo and then walked down to Phewa Lake, to the south of the Pokhara Valley, to see if I really felt ready to go on a trek. It was my idea to take this walk of ten miles return as a trekking trial and practice. It took about three hours. It felt good and so I felt confident. The lake was like a mirror reflecting the mountains. There was a steady stream of people walking and the path was pretty clear.

I met Anna and Lucy there. We sat for a while taking photos of the lake and mountains. I did a few quick sketches. We walked up further and I minded their bikes while they went for a short walk, as I needed a rest. My fitness was still pretty good but the altitude got to me sometimes.

While I walked, I was privately daydreaming and noticed the sun on my hand. The hairs made a blonde rhythmic pattern that looked quite dynamic.

I got back to our guest house, had a shower and put Tiger Balm on a few sore muscles and went to bed after writing in my diary. I caught a white moth and another strange looking flying insect and tossed them outside. We had really soft red blankets labelled *Made in China*. I had a good sleep and was up at 6 a.m. I woke the others to look at our first very clear view of the mountains around Pokhara. We ran outside as they were seen best out in the street. I went up to the roof and took a couple of photos. I followed a man who went up to a higher roof. There were fabulous views all around us.

Pokhara.

Pokhara.

AUSTRALIAN WOMEN CAN WALK

Thursday the 20th of September, I went to pay for my ticket to Kathmandu. I was advised to come to the airport early, as there was free seating and to sit to the left side behind the engine in case we could fly over Annapurna and/or Everest.

After that I went for a walk with Lucy along the road to the west to the temple on the rocks. We caught a taxi part of the way there and then walked again. We got directions from a man selling umbrellas and melons. There were many people slogging away walking uphill, slog, slog, and the very good view today of the mountains was getting even better.

At the peak we met Dave who we had met earlier today, an old man with his young boys, and Tim and Anna. I had a good conversation with Tim as we sat on a large stone looking at the view. Lucy sat next to me on the other side talking to a girl. I had sweated though my shirt and daypack.

We walked up and up and talked with many people in a village, which had excellent chai. The teahouses were open to the street but we could all sit inside as well. I had two cups of tea with sugar. I did a quick sketch of the teahouse, the kettle, the man, the small boy without pants, and a woman smoking. I was sketching a lot at the moment.

Then we continued on up the hill to Sarangkot. There were views and more views of many valleys, a lake and vibrant green hues in every direction. Then of course there were the breathtaking peaks of Machapuchare and Annapurna.

There were groups of kids at the chai shop after the peak, who wanted to hold your hand, asking for money, food, and drink. A man in a bright blue jacket yelled at them. I felt it was not safe, especially on my own to give money to beggars, as so many more people then might come and follow you. Also I had seen several times that some adults would beat a child for begging.

There were three young girls and two older beautiful teenage girls herding buffalo by waving sticks. They kept telling us

"Sarangkot up here" followed by other directions about it being inside two stone stacked walls and at the top of the street. But we couldn't really understand them.

In the end it took us about two and a half hours to go up to Sarangkot and about three hours to come down again back to Pokhara. It was about six miles each way. We didn't know the real path so then you just had to go by asking local people.

Tim and Dave were leading and had red faces as the right-side path vanished into the jungle. Tim and I pressed on through rice paddies. Everyone followed us. Dave headed off a different way and I hoped we'd see him again as I had enjoyed his company. He was a fresh person to chat with.

It was a great day. Everything about it was easy and pleasant. I bought some bracelets that were made of a stretchy plastic, which we put on and off, while we joked all the way home. They were five rupees each. There were some young boys that Tim was swinging around in the air. As he put each one down they would then run off quickly, up and down the hill with excitement. Tim put one on the roof of the chai shop. They loved playing with him and were patting him a lot on his arms and back.

We ate at the Snow Line Hotel and as we left we noticed we were gradually turning and walking into the next bay of the lake. We progressed around a spur on one side of the water and along a thin ledge. Then we crossed rivers and stood in one thigh deep to cool off for a while. We kept walking, started seeing buildings and then we were back into town.

I took some photos of a baby and some kids. I felt a bit mean, thinking that I wanted more money yet these kids were so happy, fun to be with, and they had nothing. I felt pretty middle class.

We continued walking home. There was red light on the peaks in the distance now. It was still a really clear viewing night. I thought "Pink sky at night, shepherds' delight." Maybe good weather tomorrow or a good clear sunrise. I stood on some large stones and took photos of some really blue and pink clouds.

In the grounds of the Fishtail Lodge on the way to our hotel I found myself running flat out across the open spaces, which felt good, in contrast to walking carefully with a pack on my back.

I had a good meditation that evening. I always looked forward to this at the end of busy days. It gave me an ease and boost.

There was really a lot of smoke in Anna and Tim's room when I visited them next. Now I know I had asthma. I had been noticing it for a few years and it was possibly affecting me that day walking. They and Lucy were sharing two joints but I was always a faker, and as I couldn't breathe, I went back to my room for an early night.

There was a really clear view in the morning of the mountains around Pokhara. I was thinking a trek would reinforce a lot for me. I would go on my own and hopefully have another great experience.

Flew Back to Kathmandu to Extend My Visa

ON FRIDAY THE 21st of September I was up early and there were many clouds outside. So I just meditated, had a hot shower and washed my hair. My hair was finally getting a little longer and it was going a little fairer in colour. I wanted to go home again today. Waves of homesickness came at times without warning. I wanted life to be easy and familiar so I didn't have to be brave and work hard. Then that feeling would pass and I would still really want to go trekking.

I had a breakfast of pancakes, honey and milk, rice, and hot chocolate. I had been feeling day dreamy recently but I had a clear head today. The weather this morning looked calm yet cloudy. The four of us would fly back to Kathmandu but only I would return to Pokhara.

I walked with my umbrella as a walking stick to the airport. I checked in with my ticket and chose a window seat. I added my signature to the sign-in book in the waiting room. I saw Dave again outside and talked to him over the fence. I also chatted with a nurse who had a pretty, Botticelli face who was carrying her baby and was going to Kathmandu to meet her husband's parents.

I went into the frisking room and a woman in uniform patted me down. I daydreamed, and decided I didn't want the bundle of old things I'd left in the locker in Kathmandu.

We were queuing outside for the plane on the one simple tarmac, an RNR or Boeing 737 plane, and the flight was to be forty-five minutes. I sat in the window seat over the wing and watched the amazing puffy clouds and their spirals. I could clearly see the snow that mostly covered the peaks; the lower hills and valleys were very green. I could see the meandering rivers, contoured crops, houses, and lakes. I had an orange drink, two Jatz biscuits, and two lollies.

I shared a taxi to the Star Hotel and I booked a room with Lucy again that was around the back this time. Since I was homesick today I had to have a think about where to go next, to encourage me to keep travelling. It wasn't okay to go home yet. I wanted more out of this trip. I had time. I was only spending about one hundred and fifty dollars per month so my budget was fine. I still craved the challenge. I had an impromptu lunch of muesli, curd, and fruit salad, followed later with a cappuccino and a cheese fluff cake.

I caught a rickshaw to the post office. Great! There were letters from two friends back home and Ryan! One friend had just left Melbourne for London and she had sent me her address. Ryan was letting me know he was in Delhi.

I sent a postcard of the peak of Machapuchare, which was about 22,000 feet above sea level, to friends and a letter to Mum, Dad, and *the kids* (my siblings). I rang home with a handful of coins and talked with Mum. It lasted two or three minutes, as I didn't have many coins. It made us both happy. Her voice was familiar and she supported me, asking about what I was up to. Then I was alone again.

The Tiger Balm was good. It was helping with my congestion. I was excited. My mood picked up. I had a cold, but only a cold, not some rare disease that would make me go home. I walked to New Road, the main street, business district, and Durbar Square and the roads were filled with cars. I bought some Kodak Ektachrome film for the trek.

Nepal trekking visa photo, September 1979, Kathmandu, Nepal.

I went to the bank and cashed a traveller's cheque then to a photographer, who took Polaroid instants on a tripod for passport photos for my visa. Then I took a rickshaw to Central Immigration and stubbornly bargained what I thought was a fair price for a short trip of three rupees. I took advice from the hotels where I stayed as to these prices. A woman outside the immigration office told me to come back another time, as it was Sunday. Of course it was. The next rickshaw man pretended not to have change and would not accept a fair price. So I found another who would be reasonable to get home. I was pretty good at haggling now.

I then walked around looking for a restaurant for dinner tonight and for a t-shirt for the trek. There were a few second-hand shops in Pokhara but on Freak Street I found a new one. I got it for twenty rupees and also some second-hand lattice design socks, and second-hand black Wrangler cords, made into shorts.

I had decided to send a parcel home, but after the trek, including my Japara coat, jumper, books, dress, letters, and maybe exposed films. For now they might be safer with me and I would need my warm clothes for trekking.

Walking around that day I also bought a red floral thick cotton woman's blouse with a tie across the front; like a wrap-around shirt. It was really comfortable to wear and was a bit dressier than most of my shirts.

I weighed my backpack on the luggage scales at the airport today and it weighed almost the same as I did. I walked back home in a frenzy of thought, working out what to throw out or post home. I had to lighten up my pack again. Then I did some drawing on the roof.

For dinner I ate vegetable kothay, (a platter of steamed and fried dumplings called momos). They had vegetables and bean curd inside. I also had jasmine tea and hot chocolate.

The next day I had breakfast at the Kathmandu Guest House of porridge, canned fruit salad, and lemon tea. I sat with a Tibetan guy, now from Sikkim, who I had earlier met on an east coast train from Pondicherry to Puri. I came back home and tried on the black cords shorts, wrote letters until about 1 p.m. and then had lunch at Café Jamali of banana cake and lassi. There was a girl from the States showing gemstones, settings, rings and earrings. A medic, also called Dave, bought an orange-coloured coral ring in silver from her.

We caught a taxi to the Swayambhunath Temple, the monkey temple, in the west of the Kathmandu Valley. It was quite famous and many people had told us to go there. There were about three hundred and fifty stone steps to walk up, then a large Vajra sculpture (beautifully designed ritual weapon) at the top, and a complex of statues and religious architecture that was awesome. There were many Buddhas in relief and seated as sculptures on plinths and surrounded by forest.

Buddhas on the steps at Swayambunath, the Monkey Temple.

Swayambunath, the Monkey Temple, stupa.

The view of the Kathmandu Valley was mesmerising: sprawling clusters of houses, broken up by areas of trees, and the majestic rim of the mountains in the distance. I took photos and walked around a little. The whole place felt like a Hollywood stage set that was impossibly perfect. It was quite magical. I felt really good at that moment and it was this kind of experience that washed away any homesickness for days. I looked towards our hotel area to see where we had come in the taxi. Many people were playing with kites, which were often green and white triangles that made a square.

I had a quick visit to El Bistro for a honey pancake and lemon tea. I went up to my room, washed my face, and replenished the suntan cream. I felt like giving the peace sign to all the people I passed. I was feeling happy but was also feeling self-conscious and not really a hippie, so I didn't do it.

I went out again and sat on the roof to read and did my maths, budgeting the rest of my trip. Going over my budget regularly helped my planning and decision-making. I noticed I was really smiling; so must be excited about the weeks ahead. I was looking forward to trekking, and going back to India to possibly meet Ryan, and visiting some other important cities, like Varanasi. A flock of birds flew over very low. Below there was the *honk honk* of the rickshaws and cars. The sublime sunset created a soft orange on one range, a blue in the foreground of the hills, and a unique variegated pink, orange and blue over the rest of the sky.

I took a jeep up the hill before dawn the next morning to see the sun rise and ate at the youth hostel overlooking the town. It was a calm and subtler display of colour in the sky today. I was higher up the hill, where the monkey temple was. I was drawing the kites. Drawing changed to writing, to note down the last few days. I wanted to see Ryan again, yes. I wondered how he had been in Kashmir the last nearly three months.

After travelling back to the Star Hotel and talking for a long time with Anna and Tim in their room, I gave them my home address. We agreed they would have to come over sometime. They lived in Adelaide.

I had dinner at Jamali again; lemon meringue pie, coffee scroll, cauliflower in a cheese sauce, and lemon tea. I went back to my room to tear up a few letters, organise my things, and was a bit conflicted throwing out things. Some things for sure I would throw out after the trek.

There was a great big cockroach in my bed and then under it, shriek! I caught it in a plastic bag and tossed it over the balcony. I wondered what those strange white birds were that were in the flock that flew over the rice paddies today. I got a letter from Jenny who had received her parcel and loved the beedies, coffee, etc. I wrote to another school friend I hadn't written to yet. Who knows what my friends thought about me being away. Some of them were travelling too but it was to the UK or Europe.

Nagarkot

THE NEXT DAY I had brekkie next door and met friendly Tejus again who worked there. He was squatting at my table and hatched an idea for him and me to go to Nagarkot on a motorbike. He seemed friendly enough I but didn't know that much about him and felt a bit wary.

I went back upstairs to get what I needed for a day trip. I told the others where I was going. What could possibly go wrong? At least someone knew where I was. They wished me well. We went via the Central Immigration Office to fill out an extension of my visa form and trek permit, with my two new passport photos and passport. Then we were off again. It was exciting going through the town on the motorbike.

I wanted to know more about Tejus. He had a strange existence, as he expected nothing. He had no goals, or so it seemed. He did not think about it and seemed quite vague about details about our trip and himself.

We had no information at hand to find out about sights we were seeing or heights of peaks we passed. He said a mountain was a mountain.

I thought I might be asking too many questions while we were flying along on the back of the bike.

Tejus had put together the bike from bits and pieces of his sister's bike, and it was *always* hard to start. Fortunately, it was behaving for us on this trip. He smoked many cigarettes and we drank a lot of tea. He didn't do drugs or even smoke dope but he felt *stoned* on the countryside and liked going for these rides. Did I believe him? I liked him but didn't really know him. There was a big gap between us but he was good company. There was not much difference in our interest in travel but just differences in lives.

Beautiful Nagarkot took my breath away. It was much closer to the mountains and it was stunning. I talked a lot about my friends back in town, saying that I would like to come back tomorrow with Lucy, Anna, and Tim to see the sunrise and sunset.

It was my way to show him I was not on my own and perhaps it was my way of keeping myself safe. I was nervous about this outing but had still really wanted to go. I wanted the experience of a bike ride in the hills. This was a risk but I was mitigating it I thought by not flirting in any way and talking way too much about my friends. He may have thought I was too intense.

It was nice to sit with my hands on his hips, swaying, the bumping of the bike, and the physical closeness. I wanted to be back about mid afternoon which I stated several times so he knew I didn't want to go for the night.

Tejus was caught between a few cultures and countries. He told me he worked as an engineer on planes in Paris, had travelled with work and had too many hotel nights in various cities. He said it was not a good way to see things, too much speed and pressure, when he just wanted gentleness and kindness.

As we drove slowly back into town, he asked if I would like to go to his place. I was somewhere else in my head. Conversation was interrupted as we arrived at the hotel, and he had to quickly wheel around a man in the driveway.

In reply I said that I would just like to go with my friends to Nagarkot tomorrow again. Then he said, "See you after

Pokhara" and I thanked him a few times and confirmed we would meet up again. Whatever I said I realised I was not sensitive enough in making him feel appreciated but I had only just met him. I was not sure I believed his stories. I got home in one piece, which was great!

Lucy and Anna arrived at the hotel from shopping right as Tejus wheeled off. Of course they asked me if I want to see him again. My answer was clear: "Things don't feel right so probably not." It was a great day though. Once again things just kept happening, I went with the flow but maybe needed a bit more attention on safety. I went in to meditate, as I was a bit tired.

I was really comfy in my new red floral wraparound top. I was feeling materialistic, and thinking about money. I missed the daily beautiful sunrises and sunsets, and fresh air and water of Nagarkot and Pokhara, which seemed everything to me now that I was back in this big city.

There was a TV on in reception and I hadn't seen any in so long. There was something about the Bombay Bruisers playing in the Second Test, three out of four, cricket scores, India was batting, Rodney Hogg was not so good and Donald Bradman was the best ever. There were many conversations about cricket.

There was a lot of *groovy* 60s music here in the cafes of Kathmandu and this contrasted with the other large cites I'd been in while travelling. The music gave me an expectation that this place was about non-violence. A very naïve thought.

I let my thoughts go by and they did pass by. I had random thoughts about friends at home and what I would do when I got back. Maybe I would do this or that when back. Though as soon as the thoughts were out, they were gone.

The following morning we got up early to go to breakfast to test Tim's foot, which had been a bit tender from walking. We went to El Bistro and I had lemon tea, porridge, and a banana, and then a hot chocolate. I was trying hard to convince them to use their last days in Nepal to go with me to breathtaking

Nagarkot. After a little deliberation the three of them agreed. We might go for two or three nights.

We took a taxi to the chemist in New Road as Tim had threadworm. Then we continued on to the post office for me to buy stamps and post letters. A man showed me the slots in the wall for overseas post. Then we took a trolley to the bus stop to go to Nagarkot.

As we were all standing in the mud at the bus depot, cars washed us with spray from puddles on the road from the recent rainfall. Our bus would come in a few minutes. Everyone kept telling us "Coming, coming".

We found a small shop to sit in and drank Lemu. We talked with a guy who was originally Indian but had come from Burma in 1975. His family was in Calcutta, and he owned the Sky View Lodge, which opened in one week for tourists. He had a soft nice benevolent face with thin hair on top that was quite long at the back.

We started boarding the blue minibus. Before we left I was around the back, having a puff on a beedi with Lucy. It was a lovely flavour. I put my two water bottles on my seat then threw in my bag, sat on my bag and then wrestled it up on to my lap. It was a full bus. Even the roof was full and there was a dog standing and riding on the window ledge.

The man from the chemist shop was closely watching us all with a tiny child on his left hip and a small girl in a sari and red cardigan, who sat on his left leg for a while. I was watching her too. We watched each other. She got off and then sat on the hill with two other children looking back at the bus as we drove off.

These were simple small blue buses that snaked around the mountains and at times very close to the edges of the road. I had taken these buses before and enjoyed them as the close proximity of passengers encouraged us all to chat. You got used to people pressing against you.

We were sharing this bus with mothers and their kids, women and men labourers, students and businessmen in collar and tie, crates of chickens, and a dog. There was also a young couple seated nice and close together, so close. The bus had wide glass wind-down windows, which were unusual, but great for fresh air and views. There were rolling planes and bridges crossing rivers, with people blessing themselves as they bathed in the water.

There was a very old woman with incredibly intricate long gold earrings stretching her very long thin earlobes. She also had a row of nose rings. She liked Lucy and me. We enjoyed the trip together. She and I couldn't speak so I pulled out my sketchbook and drew a quick sketch of the side of her face and neck accentuating the earlobe and earring. She loved it and we laughed and it entertained us all for a while.

I also drew pictures of the man in front, then of myself, and then patterns on shirts. "Okay" was the chorus each time I finished a sketch. I pulled out the pages and gave the sketches to each sitter. I really enjoyed connecting without speech but through art.

We arrived and walked to the Nagarkot Lodge while Lucy whistled the different movements of a symphony she knew. We had some tea and ordered dinner for a bit later. Then we walked through the town. There were many ceramic shops, chillies spread out drying on the ground and tables, and people wandering at an easy-going pace.

I was reminded I saw Tejus this morning near our street wearing a batik shirt and jeans, carrying a shoulder bag. He called out, "See you after Pokhara!" I liked him romantically, maybe? Or possibly I just liked the idea of a romance, as I really still knew very little about him.

After that we sat in our lodge's backyard surrounded by the amazing mountains. The peaks of the ranges were awesome. I didn't really want to talk. I just wanted to take it all in. We were watching the sunset while a guy with an English accent chatted away and Anna read out some science fiction. I couldn't really understand them so I went off to my room to sleep.

The next morning, Tuesday the 25th of September, there was a knock at our door. The word was that if it was cloudy we were not going to the top today. I got up early, went to the toilet, and looked outside at the layer of cloud, came back in to meditate, went back to bed, and later got up for a late brekkie of hot chocolate and porridge. When I went back to our rooms the others were ready to go for a walk.

Lucy looked white and went back to the toilet to bring up bile. I had got over my cold but now she was not well. I had to keep an eye on her and hoped she would be okay. We went back for another hot chocolate and to wait to see how she was doing. She decided we should head off, as she wanted to go for a walk too.

I talked to people as we walked including a captain and a major who were in the Nepalese army. We walked to a cheese factory and bought a quarter round of soft fifteen-day-old cheese. We met Jamie and a Swiss guy whom we knew from Kathmandu. It was really nice to keep running into people who you had met earlier.

When walking again we had to stop and sit on the bank of the road as Lucy was sick. We had an *over-the-top* chat about her health, and then met up with Anna and Tim. She was getting really anxious that something was seriously wrong with her. Occasionally snow peaks showed while I walked slowly at the back with Lucy, as she was sick in the gutter. We all stopped for a pot of tea and pancake, and a taste of a bottle of rice wine, which we all shared with the last of the cheese.

I met an American called Louis and we walked on to the viewing tower at the top of the hill. We were talking about western influences in India, habits, aspects of Hindu religion, superstitions, and that we still occasionally liked to go to church on Sundays. We met an Israeli woman with a US accent who was telling us about kosher food she had found called momos. She had grey long hair tied up in a topknot. We met a young Japanese girl-boy with a great smile who blinked a lot caused by irritating contact lenses.

From the tower we could see 360 degrees all around town and at 4 p.m. the clouds began to clear so we were encircled by layers of green, then blue, then snowy white mountains. It was impossibly beautiful. It was a spectacular moment. It was timeless. The air was so fresh. The space was so high.

We headed back down and I said my farewells to Louis, who I think I met the first time at the YMCA guest house in Madras. We both said, "See you again."

There were brilliant orange and red stripes of colour and haze flooding the clouds all across the sky, confusing the horizon. We made it back to the lodge. There was a girl that looked a lot like my older sister getting washing off the lawn where it was drying in the sun. Several snowy peaks were showing so I took a few photos. At home I didn't see much of my older sister and would always like to see her more.

For dinner I had dhal soup, a cheese and tomato jaffle, milky rice pudding, and hot chocolate. My view in every direction felt like the top of the world. The colours in the sky changed so rapidly. The yellow colour behind the hill was like candlelight.

The next day we woke while it was still dark and walked uphill to see the sunrise. We made it to the picnic place, where there were some older women who had come up in a white car. The whole horizon was clear. The snow peaks were lined up. To the right were what looked like several sunrises behind a long grey cloudbank? The light shone out, more, then less, then more, on the snow peaks. Then the brown mountains that were down below became visible too.

The three major peaks we saw the first evening were visible again, then another really beautiful one. The next peak was lit with orange light, with some white snow breaking through the colour. I had no words. So glad we came. I saw a few people I had met previously up the tower.

Back at our hotel I had a breakfast of porridge and put some of it on a dog's head for fun. He knocked it off and ate it. I grew up with a golden Labrador, a cat, and budgies. I enjoyed playing with pets but wasn't in a rush to get any as I wanted to travel.

We went back to Kathmandu.

Things I remembered from that trip back were: sick local people sitting at the UN Post where there were rows of sandbags, two wooden gates and many foreigners, like us, always looking up and watching the snow peaks. There were older people in tourist buses who were brought up to go to the Everest Lodge for a toilet stop where there was a clean, western toilet in a cubicle outside the lodge. There were farm noises everywhere all the time: turkeys, cows, birds, and cocks crowing. Then there were many kids squealing, and bus horns, as we all stared mesmerised by the majestic mountain peaks.

This bus trip was crowded, standing room mostly, but I got on and my shoulder ended up in another person's armpit, which was quite comfortable. It somehow softened his attitude to me as a tourist and stranger, and he kindly showed me when to get off the bus for the Nepal Airlines. It was a friendlier encounter than many jammed transports I'd already had on this trip. There was also a seated old Tibetan man squashed between Tim and me. As he got up to leave he pragmatically pushed off with his hands on my knee.

Back in Kathmandu, I wandered, trying to book some way back to Pokhara. On the way I saw a very brave guy pedalling energetically then freewheeling really fast from the congested traffic in the roundabout into New Road.

I eventually found seats on a Royal Nepal Airlines flight. At that office the ticket guy directed me to get my student card signed. He also asked if I knew about the festival that was on. It was a festival for Kali, the Hindu goddess who had many goats sacrificed to her. He said I should come back there at 5 p.m. and he would take me to a temple to see the animals slaughtered. I think I may have misunderstood him, but I really thought it was a funny pickup line.

5 p.m. came. Should I go or not? He was a stranger. Maybe I should be cautious. I didn't go back to meet him but shared a rickshaw back to the hotel with an American guy who sold contact lenses back home. I had to meet up and check in with the others. I got my baggage from reception and walked next door and found them in the restaurant.

Lucy looked much brighter and was mostly well on the bus earlier today too. She had been really quite white up at Nagarkot. Maybe it was the altitude.

Back up to the room, loafed around, washed my clothes and face. Our drying underpants decorated the room.

I was thinking that after Pokhara I would live around Freak Street for a few days, and visit Patan before going back to India.

I was now packing for my trek, so I didn't want to buy too many things. Then I found a bar of Pears Soap in a shop, so why not buy it. It reminded me so much of my home as Mum bought it always. I thought random thoughts about Mum and Dad, home, and all my things I had left there. I missed them but was still not ready to go home.

After thinking about my parents I began to also remember the old man called Shanti, who I met in the Sri Aurobindo community in Pondicherry. He spoke a lot about humility. In conversations with people since then I had given out his name and spoken about him as an example of people who don't eat meat, and don't do this and that. He knew little about other parts of India or other countries but lived simply for thirty-one years in the same room, isolated but content in life. He was a busy doer in their town, up early for yoga and lots of jobs but he genuinely seemed not to crave anything. The most content person I had ever met.

There was cloud cover at the moment, which made sounds seem very loud. A plane passing over roared and rumbled.

On Thursday, the 27th of September I could hear a little boy outside counting up to one hundred. Then his father said the English alphabet through and then in Nepali too. Now they were singing. It reminded me of my young niece.

I was really looking forward to my trek but had my usual anxieties about being on my own again. It was the same with Ryan. What was I to do? I had to go by myself or go home. It would be okay.

The others walked back in from shopping. I packed up, paid my bill at the Star Hotel and saw the others off. I kissed Lucy, Anna, and even Tim who was often a little distant. Tim said to me that I was "The ultimate in Feminism." We all said, "Look after yourself and see you in Melbourne."

I felt like crying so went back upstairs to the first floor. I passed the corner where a lady in a green shawl usually sat at the fourth-floor window watching. It was a sauna downstairs in the foyer at times so it was good to stay up here.

I packed and around midday went down to reception to head off. There was no one there to see me off. I made an issue of putting the key on the desk and said it out loud.

I took a rickshaw to the post office. There were two letters for Tim, and one each for Anna and Lucy. I forwarded them on to Bangkok as I'd agreed I would.

I walked to the Nepal Airlines Office and got permission to put my bag behind the counter until my flight. I saw the clerk who had asked me to go to the temple yesterday. He was a bit irritated with me. What right did he have to be like that to me? We were strangers. I did not have to do what he wanted nor apologise for it. Don't do the dominant male trip on me. I said I couldn't make it back last night. He began talking on the phone and to another customer and confirmed that "Yes your flight is for 3 p.m." I didn't say goodbye and wandered off.

I went back to sit in the lounge until 2 p.m. The same clerk came, with a young trendy couple and other intense ground staff and sat near me. He said he waited last night, as if I *was* willing, it would have been something unique to tell people in Australia about. I was glad I didn't come back. I had no trust in this guy. He said tomorrow there were also sales in the main bazaar of many goats that were all to be slaughtered and eaten.

I had asked a guy at the Garden Hotel about this festival and he said he didn't like to see all the killing, but he would gladly join in all the eating.

I caught the bus to the airport. I met two Danish girls, a French couple, a lanky looking guy in weird overalls with his girlfriend with a black ponytail in blue harem pants, and also a crazy looking agitated man in a blue t-shirt and shorts.

I checked in my bag and paid ten rupees tax. My passport particulars were written down, and then I sat cross-legged on a couch. I lined up to be frisked again at the ladies' room while they worked to get the luggage ramp conveyor belt going.

Back to Pokhara On My Own

I WAS FLYING from Kathmandu to Pokhara. Our plane was late. There was mechanical trouble with it in Pokhara. I hoped it would arrive at some time but equally I'd rather not fly on a dodgy plane.

So I chatted with a nervous American neurophysicist lecturer from Canberra University. He had been seventeen years in England or Australia. This was the first year in the last eight that he hadn't visited America. He felt caught between three homes. I wondered if I would end up like him, unsettled and caught between overseas and home. I was sitting with three giggling Indian women. One got up by leaning on my shoulder. Her husband was weighing himself, and others on the large luggage scales, to pass the time.

A girl in a khaki-coloured sari, dark green choli, and uniform jacket frisked us all. She really felt me over. It was quite confronting and a bit unsettling. I said thank you, so did she. Her eyes looked drugged, like the guy at the Nagarkot Lodge who spoke about his tin of opiate hash and yeti dog Babu.

We boarded the plane and I sat next to a professor who was scared of flying due to bad experiences in the past. He lectured me repeatedly about not eating lollies as they rot your teeth. Again…we are strangers. You are overstepping telling me what to do.

The plane ride was a little bumpy. I looked out the window at snow peaks behind the clouds that were shifting and changing. I could see lakes and green valleys inside the mountain range. We were not very far above the mountains.

When we landed we filled out arrival cards. I met a guy I knew from the Garden Hotel and shared a taxi with the two Danish girls to my hotel. Coming back to Pokhara felt familiar and I was comfortable.

There was no drinking water on arrival, they were boiling a new supply, so I just went back to my room, washed my face, and meditated until dinner. A German couple and I were the only ones there in the dining room. The woman's name was Lee or Leah. I chatted with her husband too, about their three kids, being a grandfather, and their home in Germany. I sat smiling and nodding at their very relaxed and warm talk.

I woke around about dawn, washed, and checked out the mountains. There was a wonderfully clear Sarangkot peak. It would be a good place to be today. The father of the hotel directed me to the roof to take the best photos. I sat for a while and thought about my family so far away. I remembered today was my mother's birthday. I hoped my letter had got there in time. I could taste the chocolate birthday cake and imagine the family visiting her.

Then I headed off back to the trekking office. Tomorrow I would go hiking to Ghorepani on an eight-day trek, but allow an extra two days if needed for stopping at nice places, swimming and washing in hot springs. So we wouldn't rush it. I was pretty excited. I hoped I was still fit enough. I looked forward to the challenge and the beauty of getting closer to those mountaintops. I paid for the trek, the guide's food, and a sleeping bag. I met the guide, who was a bit evasive.

I would love to have had friends here yet I was not desperate. I would go solo, in my new red floral Nepalese top.

I walked to the lake, town, village, and the falls down the road to warm up my legs. Today was a very calm day just getting ready. At the lake I hired a boat, which came with someone to row. A young boy told me many people prefer him rather than a big man. So I booked him for two hours.

When I was walking to the boat with him, I met three Indian ladies who asked if I knew restaurants with western food. It felt cool to be directing them around the next corner. I quietly said *Didi* (which means *elder sister* as a sign of respect) to them. I wasn't sure if I was being a bit familiar.

This young rower lived day to day. He told me his wage was his food of a subji or veg dish, and sticky rice. He ate, and then the next morning, there was nothing so he worked again. I appreciated my life and worried a little about his. He took me to a small waterfall. He had a blue boat that his twenty-four-year-old brother had built. His brother worked at the shipyard. He had a lot of mosquito bites on his neck.

I tried to follow his stories. He was very chatty. He said that today on bazaar day, you bought goats, took them home or to the temple to kill. He invited me to come to his temple in three days to worship, as the goat killing would be over. The temple was seventeen years old, and when the dam broke it became an island. In three days, there would be six days of big meals. Then in one month there would be another festival. On the island and behind the rice paddies you could rent a house for two hundred rupees per month.

This boating on the lake was really relaxing. We washed our hands and face at the falls and then went out into the lake, and curled around into the next bay. On the land you could do fishing. There were also small one-person canoes.

Rowing back, we passed nude and topless swimmers. It was shallow enough in a rock pool area for me to take a dip but instead I just flicked the water for another brief wash. I was getting a bit too much sun on my head. We went back to shore.

As we left the lake I saw an epileptic boy have a seizure and fall flat on his nose. A few people gathered. We put water on his head and took him into the shade. Someone said: the really strong sun stimulated the retina? I had a hot head too and wanted to meditate soon.

I was happy back here in Pokhara and it had been a mostly fulfilling day.

Walking back, I looked at the lake and loved the animals all around us. People were saying "Namaste" genuinely and looked into your eyes as they said it. There were girls working, carrying grass baskets on their backs that were hanging by straps on their foreheads. I remembered that I must be at the trekking office tomorrow at 7:30 a.m. I passed the trekking guide, couldn't remember his name, and wondered if he even remembered me. From tomorrow that would change.

Back at the hotel, I found a flea in my hair, so did a thorough check of my hair more outside on the lawn. There was a Japanese man in the foyer talking to a young houseboy and hiking Sherpa who looked a lot like Ryan. I had a tense neck and head. Hoped it would pass after meditation. I seemed to have better posture lately but was still aware of my left shoulder dip.

Then I went for a walk to Devi's Falls. I saw many people coming back from the bazaar, some with goats, and many shading from the hot sun with black umbrellas and many Indians on holidays. It was a pleasant and happy scene. I saw three women I met at the Kathmandu airport or maybe it was on a train somewhere. I had a déjà vu moment with them. I'd had so many experiences this year sometimes they did run together. Next year I could digest them but for now I was busy being there. The women and I chatted and laughed. It was nice to see them again.

At the falls I was conned by two women in their thirties. One was breastfeeding and sold me a handshake gold bracelet buckle on a belt for forty rupees that didn't tie properly. They would not give me a refund. It was tense and a man who knew them followed me to a chai shop in a slightly menacing way. I felt a bit vulnerable but it didn't throw me off too much.

I was more subdued walking back to my hotel. Then a boy wanted to sell me drugs and was surprised when I said no.

I went back home and hung out my top and undies to dry. I was drinking water and chatted, with my door open, to Satgumaree, who worked at the hotel and who was fixing the broken fan and a loose plug for me. We both had dusty feet. After he left I got packed for tomorrow.

Poon Hill Trek

ON SATURDAY, THE 29th of September, I arrived early at the trekking office in Pokhara for my departure. We caught a bus to the end of town just past the temple and started walking. His English wasn't extensive so I just followed him silently, mostly. He carried my pack while I had a small daypack. We took the path to Sarangkot.

I had to trust this man, my guide, and hoped everything was okay. The map I had was too big in scale. Over the first day or two of the trek I asked him a lot of questions. So gradually I found out that his preferred name was "T.J.", he was thirty years old, married, had one boy, and lived fifteen minutes from the trekking office, across from the airport. We were headed to Ghorepani and the Poon Hill lookout then one more day forward, and then planned to turn around and return the same way. It would take nine days.

For lunch I sat outside on a teahouse porch. I had a plate of subji, and ate from a tray of charred naan bread. They kept topping up my bowl with delicious dhal from a saucepan. There was also chai and drinking water.

We walked alongside a river and Tibetan camp, and then crossed it by planks. T.J. had a bad stomach. He was eating only curd and drinking Raksi. He talked about what he liked to drink including Raksi, a traditional distilled alcohol made from millet, or another rice wine. It could have different flavours, and was sometimes part of religious celebrations. It was drunk so widely that it had led to temperance organisations run by women.

He said to me, "You are strong" as I walked at his pace. My fitness was picking up. I did feel strong but I still dawdled *up* the hills. He asked my height. We had many rests at chai shops. There were not many snacks. I carried a few biscuits.

At one stop I sat having chai with old Nepalese men, a U.S. couple, and a baby girl called Gauri whose Mum sold us the tea. There were strings of white flags hanging at that teashop, to respect their gods. There was a pig below the window honking and making long whines.

You would meet people at the teashops, then they or you would leave, but you often passed each other again on the path. It made me feel as if I had friends even though they were random strangers. We continued along a river catching up with some of this last group of people. It then opened into plains behind Sarangkot with rice fields. I sat under a tree with a young French guy talking about other currency values, such as, francs and pesetas.

We saw a festival in one village. There was a water buffalo carcass being turned on a fire to burn its hair off. They used goats and hens too, if they couldn't get a buffalo. They then washed the char off, cut it into pieces to boil, and shared. There were often thin ribbons of this meat hanging and smoking over the fireplaces in their homes. They had two days of a big feast and party at the moment.

There was so much beauty surrounding the village. I looked back at the valley. After this we would climb up to the lake in the distance and then there was Machapuchare Mountain in the Annapurna range, at present hidden by cloud.

As well as donkeys carrying loads on the track, there were people carrying large loads of hay on their backs with forehead straps who looked like walking haystacks from behind.

We met a Japanese expedition that had forty-three people in total including seven porters. They respectfully passed us by on the path. I could see they were carrying climbing ropes, foam storage boxes, and bamboo poles strapped to their porters' heads.

As we walked along someone hand delivered to me a parcel of many letters from my friends back home. It was sent via the post office, the trekking company office, and another walker from Pokhara. I was pretty impressed with that. I felt closer to home and safer receiving this parcel. It buoyed my spirits. It took me ages to read them all but reading and re-reading them gave me something to do at night.

Our first night was in Chandracot. Accommodation was in the dormitory loft above the teahouse. They had a scattering of single wicker stretched beds where we put our sleeping bags.

I had a public wash using a rubber hose that I pulled from inside a pipe outside the teahouse. It extended enough to be able to wash my legs, face, and neck. I was told that tomorrow down by the end of town we would see a clear view of Annapurna II and Machapuchare. There they had a faucet and I could have a full wash.

There were two Germans who were washing too and had been to Muktinath, to the temple and town. Also washing was a bearded man who was interested in butterflies. There were many Japanese trekkers wandering around. They were telling me the unimportance of food; that the non-distraction of food was good and necessary. I was not sure what they meant.

I was learning some Nepali words. I was never sure if I had them completely correct: *Kakrdi* was a cucumber salad, *kalo* meant black, *arko* meant next, and *dhanyavada* meant thank you.

There was talk about Naudanda, a town coming up with amazing views and some sweet food you ate with naan bread and lemon. I had noticed today that my one early meditation had gone a long way. I felt good, as if it had lasted all day. During my night meditation it was so still that the only noises were my breath, thoughts, and some distant footsteps. Then the police came in to check my trekking visa.

I offered a banana as a present to T.J. and teased him as I handed it over, pretending to put it in pots of meat. There was a man walking around with a large blade who had to kill the animals for the meat festival. There were a few groups of people doing the same thing, preparing meats for the festival of Kali. I am told in other parts of India at this time Lakshmi, the goddess for abundance, is celebrated instead of Kali.

We walked through a new valley with a river going through it. It was a deep valley, all maize and rice crops, ready for picking. There were many people with head and back baskets.

T.J. said the next stop was where many people stayed. I looked back along the road. There were hotels on one side, rock steps all the way, then groups of farmhouses on the hill, a path down, and stepping stones over a small waterfall.

We arrived at our stop, which was a very small teahouse and lodging. There was a drunken man on the step but no one else in the lodge. It was a good idea to stay here rather than walk on to the crowded next group of teahouses. I didn't feel very tired, as it had seemed like an easy walk that day. I must have been getting stronger.

I tasted Raksi and skimmed milk and it was no good for me at all.

There were various animals being herded down the hill and eagles flying overhead. I ordered tea and sat in the balcony dormitory bedroom at a long bench table, until the light faded. I came downstairs into the lantern light. More new words that I hoped I had got right: *Di* (pronounced dye) means man, *hi* (pronounced high) means little boy, and *ban* means young girl.

There was crying and my host who was also the mum said the baby was hungry. A little boy carried in the baby to the mother. She also asked me if I wanted more of anything? There was no toilet or bath. T.J. was off visiting friends. There was darkness all around. I wanted her to go to her baby rather than helping me.

The guy who I thought was the father was in a western cotton jacket and cap on his head, and he carried in a bowl of fruit and sweets. He looked a little sick. He set up a candle on a bigger tray and behind one candle there was a photo of young baby, who maybe was dead now. The woman fed her husband and two chatting boys. He then growled at the boys, they skirted the room to go out to their bed on the balcony. It was strange the things you get used to. He was then slurping his dinner, there was Indian music on the radio and a man with a stick came in. He did not sit near me but rather he squatted and talked with the others. There was talk about grass carriers who grew into hunchbacks. Then the mother stood at the door for a moment of rest. I felt for her constant working life.

I could see the white of my skin through a hole in one knee of my maroon cotton pants.

There was a cradle in the dining room, hanging from the ceiling, and a cloth spread inside it. It was 7 p.m. and the only thing to do at night was to unwind. I went to the toilet somewhere and then went to bed in the small loft dormitory on my own.

I had slept well, waking just before 6 a.m. and gradually got up. T.J. had come in late, also slept up there and was talking to me a bit. He seemed a bit boozed. I kept my distance.

He asked if I knew I talked in my sleep? This was no news to me. He said I had been kicking and shouting. It worried him as he thought I was epileptic or something. I was glad. He might be a bit scared off from bothering me at night!

T.J. crawled over to the window and sat half outside over hanging with his knees to watch a hysterical Raksi man with a baby on his back in a shawl. He said, "Bad Deshaini festival here" as there was a lot of yelling around this village. The present new moon Kali festival always came after the Daishani festival.

I walked down the hill to wash. I took a photo of the peaks and had a photo taken of me by a U.S. guy who spoke some Nepalese. He had cut off jean shorts, a beard and round glasses, and a crazy brain. He seemed high on being friendly.

I washed then I headed down the hill. There were new hikers, and a rocky path that led to a big swing bridge.

Breakfast was a delicious cornmeal porridge that was freshly ground in front of us. The corn cobs hung in psychedelic multi-coloured rows on large freestanding frames high up in the sun; dots of yellows, oranges, mustards, reds, browns, and blacks. The Mum I met last night served me chai and chose two cobs, picked off the kernels and ground them between stone plates to make coarse meal. It was tossed into salty boiling water and was called dhindo. This was a simple, but delicious and memorable meal! I had two servings with warm milk straight from the buffalo, curd, and grainy, chunky, sugar. I watched a ball throwing game called mit game while I ate.

Then off we walked, following the path of the river up and down, often stepping on stones in the water, or on thin dirt ledges alongside it.

The ping I rode on near the millet fields.

I had a ride sitting in a ping today. It was a very high swing constructed of bamboo poles that they made each year at this time. I had seen a few of them in the open fields. It was connected to the Dashaini festival, which they likened to the nine-day long Indian festival Navaratri. The ping was in a flat area of open plains in a valley. I swung out over a millet field and there was such a great view below. It was different from a swing, more bouncy and less rigid which made it go sideways too. Again, what could possibly go wrong? I was very cautious with it. There was a lot of laughing from the locals below me when I was on, as I must have looked scared and out of control.

We walked on and found a mud brick house where they were making ghee. T.J. said it would be a long way to dinner so I should eat a big lunch. Just after lunch a very loud crazy man left the teahouse, walking around the back of the houses screaming.

The teahouses were very isolated set-ups where people sat inside and out, drinking chai, talking, and watching. I was watching a woman comb, oil, and plait her long hair. The cook passed her some meat strips for smoking over her mud stove and T.J. a burning ember to light his smoke. I saw cocks with fraying necks while flies hovered over wandering chooks and sleeping cats. Droopy red flowering plants grew outside the tearoom.

Then a young boy with a head basket, in shorts and a red t-shirt, just walked in and lay down to sleep on the floor. Near him was an embroidered pillow that read *GOD IS LOVE*. We sat inside on the floor while a woman made us tea. Lazy smoke from the fire filled the space. She had been married for fourteen years. Then she asked, "And you?" She had not anticipated a single woman.

Strangely, I seemed to be going okay with this trek. Why not, I suppose? I was relaxing with the give and take here, trying to appear mature, not letting tension build up. I had very little fatigue since I went to sleep so early each night. I was doing well with the walking and loving the views.

I wandered outside. Bullocks came along the path so I retreated up onto a rock. I saw a small group feast with chillied rock salt on the meat. I helped a family trying to get new shelves through a small doorway. Finally I made it to the top of the hill to look back at this cluster of houses, a village of three hundred people.

That night at the accommodation I was given a thick glass for hot water and another for cold. Their baby girl seemed unwell. The Dede here patiently explained to me where washing water was upstairs, how to choose beds, and the lounge location. Another form of thank you in Urdu was *shukriya*, which they used at this place and I when speaking with her. Dhanyavada was Hindi. On the second floor there were many potatoes in a stack on the floor and on the balcony, corn drying on a rack with their cobs sticking out in rows.

T.J. said, "Well that is all for today and soon there will be hot springs so maybe some swimming." We might also detour soon so T.J. can visit his mother's place for the festival day. He wanted to get tikka on his forehead. I don't really know why or if I understood it properly. So instead of following the ridge we had been on we would go down into a valley, and as he knew everyone, walk through yards, gardens, and crops. Then we would go up again to the next ridge. I thought this would be a unique experience but also hoped we would not get lost.

I showed the family Vegemite and me eating it. They told me about their cow dung walls. They heaped the dung on the floor, scraped it up the wall, and then washed it off. There were two German girls slowly walking to the teahouse with their large packs who looked very overheated.

I went to wash and spread my sleeping bag on a bed. I wasn't in a chatty mood so stayed upstairs to write in my diary for a while. After all this walking and sitting on mud brick floors I could sit cross-legged pretty easily now.

Later I talked with T.J. to order dinner. He showed me a wild chilli plant with a blue flower. There were many butterflies and grasshoppers. They woke me up with their colours and made me feel really happy.

I could hear echoing voices, cocks crowing, drums beating, and a snake charmer performing. A horn bleated out for a festival procession and donkey bells were ringing across the valley. People sang, clapped, and laughed downstairs.

In the morning I learned that we were in a tiny village called Ullepe (pronounced *you-leppy*). But I never did get the exact spelling for it so I may have misunderstood. We were halfway up a sheep herders' hill so no wonder I was getting tired walking. Everything started to run together; the walking, the views, the teahouses, and the various people.

In the lodge, T.J. tried to sleep too close to me last night so I couldn't roll over. I slept with my arms folded. He said you could be friendlier with this. I say nothing but acted aggressively back. I soon rolled over, and when I rolled back he was in the way. I showed my anger and moved his bed and him away. It was a kind of showdown. He wouldn't do that again.

I did not speak to him as I woke up. I packed up and a little later than him I went down. I was a bit freaked out at first but my anger saved me. I was lucky nothing else happened, but there were other people around downstairs and I would have created a huge fight and he knew it!

There were two German guys and one Afghan who came after dark last night. So they were also in the dorm in the morning and I was not all night only with T.J. I chatted over breakfast a little with them too. One played a flute, they shouted orders, and disliked smoking. We discussed whether we slept well. I was not so conversational as usual. One guy called Stephan wanted to come to Australia.

The boys ate the porridge but mixed in some of their own food. They carried puffed rice and some peeled green legumes.

I would have liked a day with them for company so I could speak English.

I said, "See ya" to the three guys but then they passed us as we started up the hill.

The dense forest around this area was verdant, lush, and a lovely wet atmosphere, with moss and lichens on some trees. We had to keep checking our legs for leeches, as we wore short socks and our trousers were rolled up. I threw off a big one on my hand at one point. I would love to have ditched T.J. after last night but I felt I had no choice. I continued to speak to him in a slightly aggressive way and he seemed to get the message. He kept away from me now.

We met the boys again on a bridge where they were washing in the streams. Up, up, down, down, not too tired and no muscle pain, so okay. We met again as they passed us at a teahouse. There was a nice feeling at that house; a big dog and a smoky grey tabby cat added to it. Many donkeys were passing us in a convoy loaded with bags and baskets.

Later a girl near her isolated mud brick home with blisters and a puss-filled infected hand approached us. There were no doctors around here and it looked like it needed a tetanus injection or antibiotics. It also looked like it needed to be stitched closed. She held it close to my face. Perhaps she thought I would be more helpful to her than a Sherpa, expecting I would have a first aid kit, but I did not. I realised I should have had one.

We went into her house. It had a very tidy and open main room with a shiny compressed mud floor and all bedding was in a trunk. To the left in the corner was a small built-in mud fireplace. Next to it was a wooden bowl of chunky salt and over the fire was a grill with a large, black, metal kettle boiling water.

So that was how we will do it… *garam pani sal*… hot salty water. I knew *garam pani* meant hot water in Hindi and I added the sal or salt to it, in I'm not sure what language. This was an idea and they got it. I suggested she make a paste of salt and hot water and put it on her hand overnight. During the day she could soak it in hot and strong salty water five times per day, and then dry it outside in the sun. She must keep it moving so as not to go stiff and keep it very clean. I was not sure what else to do as I thought any bandaging might not be clean. They both thought this was okay and after a little more conversation to make sure she had the idea we continued on.

The three guys passed us again and it seemed T.J. didn't like them.

We made it to Ghorepani, to Poon Hill, a small lookout on stilts. It was excellent! It felt like the top of the world and you could just reach out and touch the peaks. There was hardly anyone around and it was so wonderful to feel and breathe this amazing fresh air and almost feel as if you were floating in space. The guys were there.

After a while we headed on up the hill past the lookout area, via a different district for what T.J. promised me was "A very good meal." He had better not be playing any games or I would be extremely angry with him. He was slightly scared of me now. There were two older German men at this teahouse. We also met an English girl who was wearing a thin, red sleeveless shirt and navy shorts. She had very short hair and was very business-like.

The lunch *was* really good. As I clearly loved the food they asked if I wanted to watch the girl who was cooking. She looked about fifteen or sixteen years old and it was a friendly few minutes there with her. I sat on my jumper on a bench seat to watch.

There were chooks pecking around while I washed my eating hand in an orange plastic cup. Looking down the hill below us we were in the clouds.

We walked again; there were crows in the trees, a strong blue sky behind the clouds, small waterfalls, and swing bridges.

We were surrounded by forest all day. My t-shirt was full of sweat and I was covered in what seemed to be layers of sweat.

I had a leech bite inside my shoe, on my hand, and then in my trousers I found another one and threw it off. There were small brown monkeys and big grey chimpanzees with white faces and beards jumping from tree to tree. They screeched a little as they worked their way around the trees. I couldn't take my eyes off them. There were also men digging in the forest.

This was the day we left the ridge that the tourists took and went down a steep hill into a valley and up again onto another ridge. This gave another perspective on the peaks and there were many really great sights.

Walking down through villages and up to the next ridge.

Village.

Then came a drop of rain that woke me up. The valleys were becoming very pretty with diverse vegetation and the green more intense because of the increasing rain. We talked with a very blonde hiker who winked at me and told me he was heading to Tatopani tonight. I thought, *Bloody hell, here we go again.* I was getting a bit sick of strange men thinking approaching or propositioning me was okay.

We arrived at T.J.'s elderly mother-in-law's place. As soon as he walked in, she applied tikka to his forehead as part of the Dashaini festival and tucked a few barley shoots behind one of his ears. The tikka was a mix of vermilion pigment, rice, and yoghurt in a thick paste. Should I tell them what I thought of T.J. at the moment? They had no English and would they care? I had no idea about local attitudes on social issues.

While this was going on, I sat on a thick, coloured mat watching a young girl and baby lying there too. From time to time I took deep breaths to restore my strength after the walk. A few women were picking corn kernels into bowls.

Then we went back off again into the rain. We had our waterproof gear on. It started coming down more heavily and we got on a path that went down between houses and through various backyards. Further along we both had the realisation it was too hard to travel two hours in the rain to get to his mother's house today. T.J. talked to a local boy and after much hesitation, he decided it was impossible to go there today. I was ready for a rest too so we turned around.

We went up and up steps in that fairly steady pouring rain. T.J. threw away the barley shoots from his ear and didn't call in to his in-law's house again as we passed it. He had fulfilled that obligation it seemed. Tomorrow we would go to his mother's.

We stopped at a teahouse, rested, and I did some writing. I talked with some Germans who were going to Delhi. We were going to Tatopani hot springs tomorrow and perhaps I would get a swim and good wash. I dreamed of floating in luxurious hot water.

On Tuesday the 2nd of October I noted in my diary that I had several leech bites and was woken up a bit early by the sounds of the French girls packing. Last night I had long chats with them. They had come from Dumre, Manang, and Muktinath in Nepal and today moved on to other areas I didn't know. Their trip sounded well researched, very planned, and mostly trekking. Where was I? We were all so different. I would love to do a trip like theirs. It would have been a more ideal situation for me but I was still alive and doing okay.

Yesterday and last night there were many ladies in Chinese velveteen clothes smoking hashish and anywhere near that smoke your mind wandered. Also, I faked a few puffs with a German couple in the dorm. The guy had been a doctor for five years, and the girl had aching feet and a cherub face. I was trying not to trigger my asthma so withdrew as soon as was friendly and went to bed early as usual. I needed the sleep for walking each day. Even that small dose of hash gave me really hyper-visual dreams of an Indian person dancing. The costume she wore just kept changing to more and more intricately decorated costumes; change, change, change, and then I woke up.

T.J. didn't sleep at the teahouse dorm last night, as he didn't like hanging out with foreigners as they talked too much and he couldn't sleep then. Many hikers walked past this morning during breakfast.

What if I stop writing my diary? I wondered if I would ever read it and was wasting my time.

So we headed off again this morning without rain, down through the backyards and across the streams and rice paddies. We walked down and then up, onto the other ridge. I still felt some kind of reaction to the Germans' drugs last night, like a hangover. The walking was hard going but the fresh air was good.

We had a small lunch at T.J.'s mother's place. She was poor. There were many old ladies, "all over eighty-four" I was told, smoking chillums for hours and chanting. They put tikka on T.J.'s forehead. Here everyone seemed to smoke a lot or maybe it was for the festival?

At his village everything slowed down. We just sat. Women were picking out grit and stones from sundried dhal spread out on a cotton cloth on the floor, and guarding larger quantities of other grains drying in the street. I saw other women sitting in a circle, each grooming the hair of the one in front.

There was some light dribbling rain on and off all day. I found the villages really stimulating so I sat outside or wandered.

In the afternoon we walked again but took a break at a religious festival party. There was a large concrete paved area next to a building, open on three sides, with a roof over it. There was a huge pot full of slightly purple, milky hash or pepper chai. It didn't look like Raksi, which is more like whiskey. There were about fifty men sitting on mats, chanting, singing, and occasionally drinking the tea.

As we left there, we tried not to laugh or make silly rude comments about seeing monkeys having sex in the forest below us. I did not want to be nice to T.J. but just civil.

I met one of the German guys again. He was at the next teahouse where we stopped for chai. It was just before a swing bridge over the Black River. This river may have been the Kali Gangaki River but the Sherpa and locals called it by this more colloquial name. I was told this led to a stone path to Tatopani, which meant the hot springs were close.

We stayed at Tatopani that night. I had a room there on my own. Having my own room with a padlock was quite strange after dormitories, but it was a good strange. I enjoyed my own space again.

Over a meal I swapped addresses with the Germans. I couldn't find the private hot pools the French girls swam in and I did not have enough drive to keep walking around looking for them. At least I had washed in some hot water at the public springs with my bar of Pears Soap, so I was happy. I had learnt to be flexible as there was always something or someone of interest.

On the morning of Wednesday the 3rd of October, we were in Tatopani, Nilgiri. It was clear and I photographed the mountains. We had incredible views of the Annapurna range. It was impossible to do justice to the views, the air, and space, even if you had a wide-angle lens. I didn't know how to share this with everyone back home. I wanted to write lots of letters soon.

I heard chanting and whooping in the village. There were distant echoes of music and drumming like a war dance. It was probably for the festival season that was going on.

Today most people didn't look up as they walked by. They were serious hikers. We had extra days so we were not in a rush and had two slow days with not much walking. I wanted to be able to take the time to really soak in the surroundings rather than just hurry by.

At the river, I met a group of people, two Israeli and two French, who I had travelled with on the plane to Pokhara. I didn't recognise them and said, "Do I know you?" My mind was miles away. I should have remembered them but so much has passed since we met. What to do? I will try to explain it to them if we meet up again.

There were four Japanese people taking turns to play a tabla and a young boy playing a little Nepalese tune on it as well. At 1 a.m. that morning I had heard Nepalese music on the radio somewhere too.

I met a couple from Boston. They were in Nepal for the Big Brother and Sister community aid program but were also trekking for a month. She worked for that organisation and he was an economist.

"Anything and everything is going fine," said one of the Israeli men. He was coming up the path to have "a toilet stop." I never did see an actual toilet anywhere on the trek.

At 8 a.m. we slowly took off heading back the way we had come. We visited the teahouse, just over the river and the cable swing bridge, and we met the large, religious party that was still going. We were invited to stay for three hours and then take rice with them, as they were breaking a fast to finish their festival. T.J. and I agreed and stayed.

This country from Tatopani to Shikha had very beautiful views of distant snowy peaks and rocky-forested mountains. The village people and the butterflies were charming. Much of it was uphill. I washed at Shikha in my bikini top with my trouser pants rolled up. The Israelis nearby washed in the nude. The kids and other village and trekking people came yelling and screaming at them. I thought the whole scene was hilarious but clearly nudity was not okay here.

We saw many Nepalese and four Australian guys walking back from Muktinath, a pilgrimage site. At a chai stop a man was coming out of the teahouse looking a bit menacing with an axe handle but nothing bad happened. Along the way I bought a big lemon and four little ones for four paisa.

As we walked on I heard the familiar voice of a girl from one of the earlier teahouses. She was quite small and sick, looking up from her sister's back. She was hidden under a shawl but saw me. It was so sweet to meet them again. We had enjoyed each other's company a few days ago. Under a walking haystack, I heard another older female voice. She was a small and very wrinkly lady travelling with the two young girls. Her name was Shanti, the same name as my friend in Pondicherry. I tapped Shanti on the top of her head. She took my first two fingers and led me along in a joking way. I laughed until I was coughing.

Thursday the 4th of October, it felt as if we were on our way back. The views of the highest peaks were more distant but still spectacular. I felt very good even though I only slept a little. These views made it all worthwhile. I was very satisfied deep within myself. There was a chilling breeze from the open window of the dorm last night. I wore a heavy shirt today to keep warm.

The dormitory had been a very busy place during the night. Someone went out noisily and briefly lit a candle. It woke me up suddenly from a deep sleep. Despite the shock I luckily slept again for a couple of hours so didn't feel too bad.

I had breakfast after all the others. Having been told by the cook to "Go sit down," I went and sat on a seat by myself in a corner. It was a very basic and poor family house.

I saw a Swiss guy who I had met at Nagarkot. I should have spoken to him but instead I remained mesmerised by the Nilgiri Himal, a section of the Annapurna range of three peaks. He understood. I wanted to soak it all in. The snowy peaks were showing and we both took photos.

Then we went to visit the Dragon's Head Shrine, a local waterspout to fill our water bottles. The girls there filled their big bottles and jugs to go in their baskets on their heads. Unfortunately they then took the spout away. I had to wait patiently to use a jug someone else had. T.J. brought along the boy from the poor teahouse and made him wash his teeth and face there too.

Back in the dorm there was a lot of creative swearing. I noticed my bed had a feather mattress. I had another short doze, as it was so comfortable. Then after sitting around for a while, I packed. I noticed someone's Yak brand smokes. Had T.J. got a bed last night? Was it full or was he saving the money? I said "Namaste" and "Shanti", and left walking slowly, towards Pokhara.

We stopped for lumpy curd, called *duy* and two glasses of filtered curd, *muy*. There I met those four friends from the plane again and I apologised for forgetting them.

Next we stopped for chai in the same place where we stopped when the heavy rain was coming down a few days ago. Other friends passed us. There were ladies sifting wheat there. "It was good wheat," they guaranteed us.

Then we were off again passing others I knew, including two German girls and one ten-year-old boy. They called me liberated, independent, and said, "Après vous okay?" I did feel quite free and defended the right to be liberated as so many people questioned it.

The track was busy today; you could see people following us, and then more in front. We caught up to some who told me stories about their travels in Asia as we walked along. They had seen wild elephants, and cows with horns stampeding. Also about when one guy was sick they had to stay in a village house until he recovered. There was another five minutes of quite steep stepping so all conversation stopped.

I saw incredible varieties of lichen and fungi on the trees.

The hikers wore various coloured jackets. We all laughed as we walked and talked. I took many breaks to look back at the snow peaks. They were slowly being hidden from view by the forest. I will miss them.

There were wispy clouds and in the next mountain range there was one little peak.

It was not as I thought. I could actually see the beautiful peaks again. Later there was another breathtaking view of the stunningly beautiful, heavily snow-covered range.

We stopped for lunch at a teahouse. It was good to be back with people who spoke my own language so I could understand a bit of what was going on. One guy was play fighting with T.J. There were two sisters doing the cooking. There were Nepalese religious pilgrims outside who stared at me strangely.

Around this teahouse there were a variety of people mixed up with many very long-haired sheep: a strong thick-set man, another with two thin plaits, another with curly black hair and an older English couple taking photos, a German mother and her ten-year-old son, five Israelis, and one Australian guy younger than me. There was also a holy man smearing a fine powder on his followers. And me? I seemed to be in the way of the photographers trying to hang on to the last of the stunning mountain views. I felt really good. The trek had been an amazing experience.

That afternoon we arrived at The Poon Hill Lodge, which was packed, but we were told we would all find a bed there so I booked in. On the grassy field out front, trekkers played soccer with small boys who smelt the tiger striped shoes of one guy, hunting him, until he fell and hit his head.

While we talked and laughed our meal numbers were called out. There was a kind of camaraderie from coming down out of the mountains. I went to bed while many sat around the fire.

I got up to go to the toilet during the night. Always a challenge finding somewhere in the dark but it was stunning outside. There was a beautiful, brilliant moon and many intensely bright stars. I felt full of energy and inspired.

On Friday the 5th of October, I had a good departure handshake from two trekkers and remained reading Ouspensky. They asked if I was ready to go but I wasn't. We agreed to meet at the Tikhedhunga chai shop after coming down from another hill they were off to see today. As I watched them go I could see a head of black hair like a mop moving around in a field of maize nearby.

Later as we walked, we met a Swiss guy who lived in a community nearby. I also watched dozens of people carrying rolls of straw mats on their heads. They faded as brown dots into the distance.

I watched the cooks make bread dough and then divide it. Half would be made into bread, and the other half a paste, which fermented into alcohol, and then milk was added to make a drink. It was a blackcurrant colour and might have been that drink for the religious festival we saw near Tatopani.

Earlier that morning T.J. had woken me up to walk to see the dawn panorama from the Ghorepani Poon Hill viewing tower. There were a few others also walking in the dark on the grassy slopes asking each other "Are you going up there?" We were about ten people in total.

In the sky above, below, and behind us, there was a pink haze with a rippling blue in it. As the sun dawned, we were in the wooden viewing tower. There were banks of fluffy clouds and soft mist over the peaks. The sky seemed bluer in contrast to the more three-dimensional white softness of the snow and brown peaks. The clouds would part and the majestic mountain peaks loomed forward to meet us. The dynamic clouds carried with them a red and grey haze that sprung forward at you visually as well. It was magical and breathtaking.

Pink and blue sky.

Ghorepani Poon Hill views.

Ghorepani Poon Hill views.

This is what I had wanted from the trek and I was not disappointed.
To-day,
too-day,
I sit here silently,
I sit in a pumpkin vine garden on my Japara coat,
looking.
People told stories about their trekking while in the tower waiting for the precious glimpses of the peaks. There were amazing tales about the names of some of the mountains. I remembered one about Mt. Machapuchare. They said that Shiva lived in the cradle on the top and so no one can climb that peak or you would disturb Shiva.

Another guide and an English guy were good company, telling funny stories. They had trekked on a small peak and foolishly didn't have their ropes out and ready, so they had to use their hands in the snow and rocks to crawl along. They called out to the group leader for the ropes from the packs. He dropped back to get them but the strong winds blew everything out of his frozen hands. They couldn't go ahead and had to stop to chase down their supplies. They chased cups and bowls all over the mountain in the snow and blizzard wind. They had us all laughing.

We headed off. It was a really pleasant day passing back down a familiar path. We were in the bush a lot of the time, crossing over streams, near waterfalls, some deep pools, and some stunning brown striped rocks.

Then we walked into the sun coming over the rise to a small town. The Swiss guy was there again and good company.

I watched some local girls swapping flowers and making necklace chains by linking petals. Then I headed off downhill in the lead. We passed a very old man going to Birethanti. We followed the river and met the French couple washing themselves and some clothes. I really enjoyed this diverse and pretty scenery of people and nature intertwined.

We saw herds of donkeys grazing that seemed very still and somehow strange and hyper real. I was aware of a feeling of being really still inside. As we walked I saw cows as well. From a distance it had seemed as though they were donkeys too.

At the next lodge only two French were staying there and they had bad stomachs. Here I washed some clothes and walked towards the next bridge for a chat with the really good-looking bearded French guy.

I saw a local boy limping along who had puss coming out of an infected sore on his bare foot. It was like the woman earlier with the infected hand; there was no doctor, no soap, and only our salt medicine idea. I asked T.J. to tell him what to do with the salt. This reminded me that on the way down from Ghorepani we had visited the woman with the infected hand. It looked much better. It was clean, she could move her fingers, some dead flesh had come away and there was new flesh healing up. I was pretty happy about that.

Later I unpacked some of my warmer clothes as it was turning cold and then sat inside for chai. I learnt *bati* meant lamp. I felt I had been faking a lot today and I wrote *vanity of the movable*. Not sure what I meant. I wore a terry-towelling hat and wrote by lamplight in the loft dorm room, as there was thunder and lightning, continuous rain, and heavy overcast clouds outside. I wrote *seeking clarity* and went to bed.

Saturday the 6th of October, I woke up at 6:30 a.m. and decided to sleep in, sure, really, why not, do nothing to provoke any discussions, and lie low. I surfaced at about 11 a.m.

A European man came and looked in at the accommodation in that teahouse. He thought it was dirty. He was calling out demandingly for chai and biscuits. I drank my hot lemon. There was also a German outside, making judgements about the teahouse loudly. I learnt *miti* meant sweets.

I was having a really easy day. We walked on and had a late lunch at Ama Lodge. It was local Nepalese food, not a tourist trekker meal.

There was heavy rain after that so we stopped again at a lodge before Naudanda. Coming down to this lodge I met two German girls and a Brisbane guy who were heading up where we had come. They were happy people, which was refreshing. These three trekkers and I admired and complimented each other for being more or less *together*. They had red dotted foreheads. They received this tikka from a Saddhu further downhill. They encouraged me to find him to get some tikka but T.J. said you only should do it in the morning.

I then heard some creative swearing from Raphael, one of the French; imitating someone else he had heard discussing some Nepali beliefs. They had apparently said, "Only men can plow." It all didn't make much sense to me but he was very entertaining.

While in the lodge there was a massive shower of hailstones. There was also continuously changing dramatic light flashes and rolling thunder. When it was over, you could see the Annapurna mountain range again. The powerful storm cleared the air and infused the atmosphere with freshness. It was exhilarating.

The couple that owned this lodge were young and friendly. The rattan beds in the dorm were new. She showed me her collection of many saris, and he raised his eyebrows, inviting any new topic to discuss rather than saris. It looked like a new generation coming through.

Back to Pokhara

ON SUNDAY THE 7th of October there was a stunning sunrise and the moon was still up. Sunrises seemed to be full of optimism for me. I played cards for a while before we headed back to Pokhara. The hills around there had a backdrop of the stunning Annapurna range whenever the clouds parted.

We walked over a bridge and up a slope away from the river. There was an occasional shower of heavy rain that we hid from undercover.

My diary has become habit-forming.

I could hear someone playing recorder scales.

There were basket-laden donkeys passing us.

There were no meals or tea stops.

I talked with Rosalie, a tall English girl from Coventry, who told me that donkeys had big ears and small, grey bodies. Mules were donkeys crossed with horses.

A loaded porter boy who passed by had an incredibly beaming and youthful face.

We caught the local bus to the airport. Mid afternoon I arrived at the Hotel Garden in Pokhara. After the busy time of the trek of nine nights and ten days, I had time to write, about yesterday, tomorrow. I had time to write about today. I was thinking I might go a few days earlier to Delhi as I was getting excited about travelling again.

There was really nice tasting water to drink here.

I learnt *tikcha* meant all right or okay.

I kept thinking *N'oubliez*, which means *do not forget*. The trek was over but I did not want to forget it, what I'd seen, and where I'd been. I was thinking about all this in a Leonard Cohen voice.

On Monday 8th October I was told it was a bad day for the Nepali. They wouldn't fly today and children got an extra holiday. I was not sure what this meant.

There was a funeral fire by the last river before the Tibetan camp, after Suiket. There was a lot of ash flying from it and the smell of hashish too.

I bought a bus ticket to Kathmandu instead of flying. There was a roof created by dozens of umbrellas being held by the line of people waiting for tickets. I walked under it and waited there enjoying its benevolence. There was a singer, pigs, sugar for sale, and huddled, homeless friends asleep close together on the pavement.

I'd had some really satisfying experiences lately but I wanted more. I felt emptiness as *the trek* was over. I think I was reading too much philosophy again and also reading about Mentalism; people who think they can do things with their minds.

I met two Scottish doctors with amoebic dysentery who were going to Brisbane. I had met them before in Pahalgam, Kashmir. I explained to them how to get a visa extension and how to visit the tourist office to work out their next travel steps.

I was doing that too. I was researching Burma, Darjeeling, Kurseong, and Kalimpong; figuring how much time and money it would take. I had a tentative flight to Patna, had priced to Calcutta, and a Thai visa. A friend back in Melbourne, Mikey, had written that she could meet me in Thailand in December if I was still overseas and wanted to meet up.

Back to Kathmandu

On Tuesday the 9th of October, I woke at 5 a.m. The cook called Pop had forgotten to make my early breakfast. I headed off, leaving during a heavy downpour again. I liked rain as it cleaned the air but now it was a bit too much. I waited under my umbrella then went to a chai shop.

An Australian couple from my hotel headed for the same bus. Louise was from Box Hill and a photo librarian. Her partner Alistair from Middle Park was a journalist. They had been working in Iran. I talked with them all the way to Kathmandu in the back seat of the bus. It was great to have two Melbourne people who were really interesting too. We talked at the toilet stops, had chai together, and shared food, and a delicious mandarin. We planned to meet again.

When I arrived in Kathmandu I went to the Poste Restante, there were letters from Elizabeth, a good friend from home, the AUS manager from Calcutta, and Ryan, who may be in Nepal.

I hoped to stay in the Freak Street area but The Century Lodge was full. They sent me to the Oriental Lodge, in the same courtyard.

I hoped to meet Ryan and sort out some future travel plans while waiting for him here. I had a funny tummy so I took two homeopathic tablets.

I went out to eat but meditated first. I felt the still part of my mind was like a continuum. It was always there whenever I needed it or took the time to stop everything else. My body got a rest but my mind got itself. It had been a huge and beneficial part of my travel.

In a shop I saw Marlborough Red cigarettes with hash being sold for one rupee each. I was still amazed how there were drugs everywhere. It was so out in the open.

On Wednesday the 10th of October, I had a hot water shower. What a luxury! Outside there was continuous rain, like winter at home. It was comforting.

I enjoyed reading and re-reading my letters. I had one from Elizabeth, an old school friend, who I had written to earlier. I was talking to Louise on the bus about her, as she also worked in news media. My school friends were like sisters.

I read any book I could find in the hotel bookcases including a few about reincarnation and theosophy. From the courtyard outside I heard the cooing of pigeons alongside James Taylor songs, the *Déjà Vu* album by Crosby, Stills, Nash and Young and the song "Rose Coloured Glasses" by the Raspberries.

I was feeling pretty free. I wondered what I wanted though. I'd like to meet Maharishi, the founder of the meditation that I do. I wanted to know the future, ride a bike, and swim better, and get into an extended relationship. Was I past it? Shanti, my older wise yoga friend from Pondicherry, thought I was too independent, so didn't need a partner. I had told him I had never had sex or a real relationship yet. My friends thought I had hooked up with someone once at a party, but in reality, he had thrown himself at me and I had slipped away.

I had a lot of male friends but didn't really like anyone that much. Some friends thought I was sexually active, some thought I was gay as I didn't sleep around, but I was just a quiet person really. On this trip with my short hair, wearing no make-up or jewellery, I didn't expect to improve the situation. I just wanted to be safe and not attract attention.

I was enjoying what seemed to be my *free will*, which I had been reading about. I *willed* myself, whatever that meant. I *willed* myself to go to extend my visa, to the Post Restante to get another letter from Ryan, to the Nepal Airways to book a flight to Patna, to wander back to the Oriental and meet Louise and Alistair, and to talk about art school at dinner that night at the Blue Bird. What is free will, more than a thought?

The last few days had been quite unreal, very full, stimulating, no stress, and it felt like things were just flowing.

My flight from Kathmandu to Patna would be on Friday the 19th of October. The bus was at 7:30 a.m., and flight time 9 a.m. I had to wait eight days for it though.

I wrote to Ryan who was in Delhi, and wouldn't be coming to Nepal now. I wrote to the State Bank of India in Calcutta again, to tell them when I would arrive to collect my money transfer they were still holding since before Nepal. I replied to all my letters, done, done, and done.

Kathmandu

ON THURSDAY THE 11th of October I wrote that last night I had met a guy named Nolan at the Blue Bird. He had collar length dark brown hair and a kind face. We shared two bottles of beer and were walking around the city afterwards. He forgot his bag in the restaurant so he ran back for it. He was a Canadian who was also travelling on his own. We decided as we were both stuck in Kathmandu for a while that we would do things together for company.

We sat on some temple steps. We made a joke of having a joint made of plain grass picked from the paths nearby. We thought we were pretty funny. He was not into drugs much. I liked that he wasn't a spaced-out person. We walked to the Mellow Pie Shop, had tea, walked home and with our hands in our pockets, we had a kiss. This event did surprise me. Maybe it surprised him too. We both felt this liaison wouldn't continue long-term but it did feel good to have a friend for a week.

This morning I met a French couple that I knew from trekking but they were flying home today. I was walking around and around to pass the time. A pigeon sat on the rung of my window. It had purple and dark silvery feathers on its neck. It was stepping around for a while, and then with some flapping it took off. I went back to the Poste Restante office again and retrieved a letter from my older sister. I did miss her and my family. I seemed so far away from them all. I was walking around the back streets through to the market.

I saw Tejus with another girl. He had not gone to Europe as he told Anna and Tim. His stories didn't stack up.

I tried the Nepali Restaurant. I could handle this city but I would like to move to the more upmarket Century Lodge in Freak Street if possible. Several people told me it was a good place to stay and my two companions from Melbourne, Louise and Alistair, were staying there too. Originally named Jhochhen Tole the locals renamed the street due to the freaks or hippies that came here in the 1960s, as marijuana was legal and sold in government shops. In the 1970s this all changed but there were still a few hippies but now more trekkers and tourists as well. I walked around the Durbar Square area aimlessly. I had a look through an art print shop at the corner of Freak St. and Ganga Path. There were many faces to say hullo to.

I took a detour to an open area of vendors. I kept looking out shop windows, watching for Nolan. We agreed we'd meet again today. Then I saw him sitting on the temple steps talking to a small boy. He was waiting at our rendezvous spot. I felt really happy about hanging out again.

We walked around the slums then decided not to buy bananas but go for some pie to the American Pie Shop.

What could we do? We walked around and back to the Kathmandu Lodge and were relaxed which I liked. It was a nice feeling to have a friend for a few days. Alas, as I got up to go to the toilet, he accidentally called me Wendy. I had to correct him that I was Veronica. That burst my bubble a bit.

I really liked Nolan as he was intelligent but also seemed easy-going but really I knew nothing about him. We went dawdling around. We were looking at jewellery and standing in an intersection when Alistair tapped my arm as he walked by and into Joe's, restaurant, saying jokingly, "I'm really into dope, man."

I walked Nolan back to Durbar Square where he told me he was going to fly out soon to see an old girlfriend. Apparently our two days together had reminded him of her. We had a few warm friendly moments. I'd love to have hugged him more, but with a pragmatic goodbye kiss and hug, I said in a definitive way, "You enjoy the rest of your trip." Romantic music bled up the hill from the central town square.

He wanted to meet me again despite me casting him off. That was... *nice*? He said he would wait on the temple steps again tomorrow. I didn't think I wanted to, but I said, "I'll look for you too."

I went back to my room. I was thinking, *Des choses a faires*? (Things to do?) I occasionally thought in a few broken French words at the moment. This stint on my own in Kathmandu reminded me of two weeks I'd spent on my own in Paris two years ago. I was backpacking with my friend Mikey who had to go back to university in Melbourne.

There were lots of things to do. I could go to the bookstore, the market at Durbar Square, to the ancient city of Bhaktapur, the market road near the Kathmandu Guest House, the Burmese consulate, and visit Patan, the third largest city in Nepal.

More Kathmandu

I DID MY washing and the day quietened down in my head. I was reading *Theosophy and the New Psychology* by Annie Besant, about thought power. I took notes about what I was reading. She wrote: "Thus we may learn to utilise these great forces that lie within us all and to utilise them to the best possible effect." I thought we create our own situations. I was also reading Annie Besant's *Man and His Bodies*, J. Krishnamurti's *At the Feet of the Master*, C.W. Leadbeater's *Man, Visible and Invisible*, and *Thought-Forms* by Besant and Leadbeater.

Forgot to wash my feet.

What was for thee will come to thee.

So many cultures talk about three aspects as being fundamental:

Christianity terminology: God the Father, Son, Holy Spirit,

Ancient Egypt: Osiris, Horus, Isis,

Hinduism: Brahma, Vishnu, Shiva,

Perfect people:

Indian Hindus call them Rishis,

Buddhists call them Arhats who don't need to incarnate in human form again unless they want to,

Christians - just people made perfect,

Theosophy - Adepts, people who had learnt all that can be learned in human existence.

What do they mean by perfect?

It was raining, a storm was breaking and maybe Nolan wouldn't leave, and I would look for him tomorrow. This mood reminded me of crushes when I was at school. It had more to do with me than the guy. I was looking for company.

On Friday the 12th of October, frustratingly, there were still no single rooms in the Century Lodge. I went to the hospital for a Cholera injection that was due.

I went to Patan, to its Durbar Square and chai shops. I took a pedicab to Pulchowk Gate and returned the same way. There were many terracotta ceramic pots drying in the square. I saw a large rat squashed on the road and many orange-coloured goat carcasses and heads in a shop window. There were many people topless having their backs massaged with their backs facing into the street.

When back I walked from the post office home, then to the main roads to the Star Hotel area. I traded my books in at the second-hand bookshop.

I had a slice of hot banana pie and apple pie with chai and chatted to an English woman who had her twenty-one and twenty-three-year-old daughters with her. She was an artist, a painter, and had travelled overland and was now organising them a trek to Annapurna base camp. I was interested to hear about her plans, as I had not gone that far on my trek. I did not want to be too remote on my own. She was a really positive person who described herself as lucky. She was much younger than my Mum as my parents had children a bit later due to WWII. She had a boarding school headmaster husband. I had no dinner, as I was so full of pies.

On Saturday the 13th of October I started the day with lassi and enjoyed a very sunny couple of hours. I bought a packet of biscuits and found some people at that shop who seemed to me to be too polite and friendly with each other to be a family, but they were.

I met Louise and Alistair and again we chatted for a long while. I might go with them to the casino. I didn't really know anything about gambling. They had a bottle of 40% ginseng.

I was reading Kafka's *The Metamorphosis and Other Stories*. I went upstairs to read, and write to my mum, and others. I went downstairs to post letters. I wandered for a couple of hours. "Exercise each day" was a good idea written by Ghandi. I was thinking about being alone and bought a Newsweek and headed back for a cappuccino. It was hard to keep up with world news this year but there was the usual mix of coups, violence, the Pope had visited the White House, and the Australian Government had abolished trade preferences for Britain.

AUSTRALIAN WOMEN CAN WALK

There were three Australians talking in my hotel lounge and still I had no friends for dinner tonight. I was the image of aloneness. Why were all my friends back home? Anyhow, I might meet Ryan soon. At 6 p.m. I washed my clothes and my lungi sheets.

I was reading in my room and making notes: create your own situation, while creating the best position for further evolution at the same time, self-image was a thought, a situation, environment, you, me, and all were in it.

Then there was a blackout. I went down to get a candle. I saw a boy doing up his forgotten fly and thought no one could see him in the dark. The lights switched on and off again. I went up again and meditated. I again felt the pull to go back home to Melbourne but it was only a fleeting mood.

I said to myself: "Trust yourself" and "Nonviolence." I believed that being anxious was being violent to yourself. I went out to dinner.

I had dinner at Joe's and spoke with a few people. There was a Canadian couple who left early, an Italian nonviolent vegetarian interested in Jainism and a temple in Calcutta, and an English guy who worked in Australia but had travelled in Southeast Asia since 1973 and showed me some of his black and white photos. There were two Australian girls in shorts from Tamworth who were tripping, dieting and yet trying to fatten up as well. A man came out of the back room while doing up his fly. Coming out after him was a big European girl. He was smartly suited and mean looking like a gangster. There were many Australian voices loudly talking about going on a trek. I was gauging the various personalities in the room.

The next day was Sunday, and I needed an outing. I took a long walk past the Palace to Pashupatinath Temple on the Bagmati River, where it met the Ganges. I watched funeral ceremonies and their fires: the bodies were loosely covered in yellow cloth, put onto wood pyres, lit near their heads then more wood was stacked on.

I walked to the Boudanath Stupa on a small mountain out of the city area. There were beautiful clouds all around. I sat for a while and then set off walking round the slopped edges there. There were many coloured flags.

I took the public bus back and then walked past the post office to the Mellow Pie Shop. Cake was my comfort food. The two Tamworth dieting girls were in a neighbouring booth there with a New Zealand guy. The lights were going on and off. I drank too much tea so was very speedy. The two Scottish doctors were in the pie shop too. I went back for a short meditation which was a little affected due to all the tea.

Then I went out again to Joe's Restaurant where I met a few people I already knew. There was an English guy who worked in Australia at times too. There was a very buff heavily tanned guy who shook hands with everyone when he arrived. Then there was a big blonde Aussie with pale skin. Standing opposite each other, these last two looked like the yin and yang sign.

And we all happily talked a lot. I chatted with this last Aussie called Matteo. He had published two thousand copies of a personal development book for two hundred and fifty dollars. He wasn't overtly spiritual and seemed genuine. It was a lovely, lovely time. We all moved on to a concert, then visited Matteo's friend, waited while he bought a coat, and then went to another friend's hotel lounge.

We all sat cross-legged while we told Nepal stories, talking and talking. I liked hearing the peace song "If I Had a Hammer" by Peter, Paul and Mary. At midnight we all went to a cake shop party and there were lots of people there, having drugs, booze, cakes, and tea. There was something for everyone and I felt really happy again.

As we all wandered home to our hotels we went through an empty, deserted Freak Street. There was a thin strip of stars in the sky. As we all split up there were various farewells like "See you in Rome." Several people were locked out of their hotels. We saw an Australian girl who had the shakes and a pain in her shoulder getting into an ambulance.

As I went off to sleep, I thought about the various friends from tonight. Matteo, who was going off to Pokhara, was a genuine person but loony too, but in a good way. He reminded me of Ryan, so energetically attractive, and intense. He'd had four spoons of sugar in his small glass of tea.

I had a look at Matteo's book. It was about keeping yourself clean outside and inside. The book had a nice format, the words were poetic, and they had a gentle softness. He encouraged working on yourself, but not in a professional way. My diary was quite rough, raw, random, trying for no hang-ups. Thinking about his book reminded me to clean my teeth.

The next day I posted postcards home. There were no letters for me and I was still waiting for the Kandy letters that had been redirected. Maybe I would never get those. There was groovy music everywhere.

I took a pedicab to near the Burmese Embassy and arrived as it was closing. I was too late, but the man there gave me my passport back anyhow as I didn't need a visa now. I had decided not to go to Burma. You could only get a seven-day visa and go to limited places. It seemed problematic on my own. I didn't want to get stuck there.

I followed a curving street and wandered a different way to Durbar Square where I sat in a courtyard for a while looking at semi-erotic temple carvings that I found unsettling. I met the Scottish doctors again. I saw some really great slim pyjamas in a brilliant blue with a red sash, but didn't buy them, as I wanted to keep my pack light. I visited the Temple of the Thousand Buddhas and got a view over the top of the shops of Durbar Square and all the town's houses.

Walking back, I sat on the temple steps again. One carved from a solid piece of rock was only for Hindus, and the rest of them seemed to be from wood. There was a sort of angel on its pillars. Buddhist temples often seemed to have two lions outside and had a monastery and chanting inside, presided over by Lamas.

I was looking forward to my hot shower tomorrow.

Today was a distraction day:

Chai was really good in the little shops,

I'll get a pedicab back to MOM's Restaurant,

The Nepali guy who worked there was friendly if you were on your own,

Which was okay for me.

I wrote to an artist from back home; wrote about Kathmandu, Nolan, Matteo, and trekking. She was a married American-Australian friend from art school and would have been a great travelling companion, but she was unable to head off and leave everything.

I had so many friends at home and so many friends while travelling. I couldn't possibly keep up with it all. I went back to my room; Louise was there, looking for me to return a book. We had a chat then I was back to writing my diary and plucking my eyebrows.

Ah, Matteo, I can't believe we ever met. It felt like a great brother and sister relationship, which was such fun. I didn't think we would meet up in India. I had a thought that maybe during this trip I had learnt to be open to fall in love a little bit with every fella I met. I was enjoying everyone's company along the way. I was also trying to feel the vein, the streak, the mood, and the layer, that seam of life that was in Nepal at that moment.

Principle of vibration:

nothing rests,

everything moves,

everything vibrates. Whaaaaaat????

I was reading so many weird books.

The trek did establish some things for me. I felt that I was not so worried anymore, though I was still very cautious.

I thought about the past and if I didn't comprehend something fully it came into the present.

I wrote to one of my art school lecturers.

I had dinner at the Tibetan Lost Horizon. There were a group of musicians in this little street, sitting near big, beautiful cows. I met Alistair and Louise again. They were so easy to talk with. They told me they would go to the casino maybe tomorrow and I should come. They told me to get a casino pass and coupon for the shuttle bus from the Hotel Crystal, and meet for drinks tonight in their room at the Century Lodge in an hour, at 10 p.m. I was not really interested but it was something to do. I had never been to a casino before.

We sat up drinking whiskey and Limca, learning about each other as we told stories. I had been drinking less and less on this trip. It was hard to keep up their pace. I told the little that I knew about Rosicrucians as they asked about it. I knew two friends who practiced that. They got manuals in the post, followed lessons, read from various authors about the mystery of life, and visited the Rosicrucian Centre on North Road in Ormond.

Then I said that I also practiced meditation. They somehow talked over me when I said that. I let it go, as they were clearly not interested in it.

We changed over the topic to our families. Louise talked about her sister and mother who wrote sincere letters to her, always offering advice at the end. Alistair was one of four boys and two girls. The first girl was adopted, he was agnostic, an anarchist, and drank and smoked heavily.

Later I walked home. The Oriental was open. As I walked past, the front desk fella was playing with his toes. I cleaned my teeth and went to bed. I was still up at 2 a.m. I drew in one book, and wrote in another… trust yourself, no anxiety, to India.

We had all discussed ideas about breaking away from others, due to their competitiveness in life and how we shouldn't care what other people thought. Our conversation seemed a bit stilted after having recently met Matteo, who had a natural sense of unboundedness emotionally and socially.

I have really liked meeting lots of different people on this trip and felt a wonderful closeness with them at times. I remembered Shanti from Pondicherry who said when he met a new person he felt dubious. He always thought about what the stranger may want and was careful. He gave me advice to take care with new people. I thought I was pretty risk-averse already.

I slept late the next day. I had drunk too much whiskey, was hung over, had pains in my hands, and dehydrated. My hot shower was great and I washed my hair, as the water flow was really consistent. At breakfast there were the three French, who usually sat outside, at a nearby table and I struck up a conversation with them and some other girls there. They were super-chatty which I liked.

I was thinking about what to do today; go to the Hotel Crystal, post office, and Nepal Airways. I had two days to go until my flight, had two hundred rupees left, and twenty book loans still out from the second-hand bookstore. I could change my money to Indian rupees so no need to spend it all.

So I got the casino pass at the Hotel Crystal, reconfirmed my flights at the Nepal Airways, and bought some travel snacks. I intended to return all my second-hand books but instead got out a few more including Aldous Huxley's *Brave New World* and Krishnamurti's *Commentaries on Living, Third Series*.

I went back to my room and was doodling in my diary. I couldn't get in the mood to write to friends at the shop where I worked last year to save for this trip. They were really nice people but we were on a different page. I decided to have one book just full of sketches. In two more days I might see Ryan or Matteo in India. If I didn't meet Ryan then I would go straight to Rishikesh.

I went to the Tibetan Restaurant then back to my room and wrote to my old work friends. I felt as if I was living several characters in my life and my letters took different angles because of that. I had written to about thirty people so far but this was difficult. I would not go back to my old job. I would go to do my teaching certificate. I think everyone assumed I was still travelling with Ryan and Adrian, as I had not told them otherwise.

Louise and Alistair came and got me. We ran to the casino bus, got in the side door, and sat in the back row. I did not note the name of the casino or even where it was as we all chatted busily on the bus. The casino had very flashy lights as we entered and we filled in our coupon at the entrance counter. Two girls gave us a tour. We settled at the roulette. I watched Louise and Alistair playing and a huge guy dealing. They were so easygoing as a couple, no problems about me being along. They said why should there be? They seemed so secure in their relationship. We played keno that was like TattsLotto, with twenty drawn out of eighty. I bought us beers. I wasn't interested in losing money so didn't gamble.

There was Dylan music playing and then some old Pink Floyd. We went upstairs for blackjack and pontoon. Louise won at blackjack but they raised the stakes to two hundred dollars so she pulled out. They got free drinks while they were playing. There was a really happy, always-laughing waiter. Also playing pontoon were the longhaired French from my hotel and the curly haired Afghan man I met a few days ago. He lost a few stacks of chips and was cashing traveller's cheques, seriously caught up in it all. And *that* is what I am not interested in.

Downstairs everyone lost a lot on slot machines. Lucky Alistair was given ten rupees too much in change. Louise was thinner, more petite, and smaller than me. I was watching and analysing the unusual people all around us on the slots, counting how many machines there were, and then we all tumbled into the little red bus to go home.

We went back to their room. We drank more whiskey, Limca, and played cards. I kept score. At 5 a.m. I had to make a guy get up again to let me out of their hotel and also another at my place to let me in. I slept well, and had breakfast at 3 p.m. This was a weird schedule for me.

I was faking it a lot that I was cool. I was going along with it all last night but I thought I was way too *straight*.

It was Wednesday the 17th of October. I finished a letter to another artist friend from home, about her birthday, my trek, Indian temples, the caste system, dowry, and marriages. I went out for a little walk to post the letter. I was thinking about changing my money back to Indian rupees, buying cheese for Ryan as a present, and presents for family back home.

With breakfast so late it still seemed like morning. Around 5 p.m. I meditated and went downstairs to read *Brave New World*. It was good fun, sitting with various other people in the reading corner.

The sun set and the lights went on. I was buried in this novel. I had another coffee. They played Dylan and the *Animals* album by Pink Floyd. It had a pig flying on the album cover, which I had at home. It was soothing to hear music I liked. I looked at myself in the mirror as I passed by it. I pretended to share a joint looking at myself, spoke no words, and there were tiny black insects buzzing around the mirror area so I walked away. I sat with Peter from New Zealand who was booked on the same flight as me on Friday.

Louise and Alistair visited, which was very nice. Louise gave me her address and said she would be home in November. She would be interested to come if I had exhibitions. We talked about our days spent together. We decided they were "Good parties." I really liked them the most of all the people I met travelling. I hoped I would see them again.

They were going back to Pokhara tomorrow, but I wasn't. I think I gave them the impression I would meet them there, but I couldn't keep up their pace of partying. They liked to go out all night and then get up after midday. I told them about how I had read a couple of articles about non-involvement. Also that I felt my Dad had it right as he wished everyone well.

I hit my head on a concrete doorpost, which distracted me during our goodbyes. The café in our hotel lounge closed. We talked about how we had noticed travellers bringing beggars in here to eat with them. I was joking about whether I would ever meet up with Ryan again, generally criticising people and not watching my tongue. I don't think I was really myself around them. I was trying to be cool.

On Thursday the 18th of October I woke about 8 a.m., meditated, washed my face, ate an apple, and finished reading a book about suicide. There was no muesli today.

I paid my ten-day bill for accommodation plus four hot showers, for ninety-two rupees. This included one hot shower that I would have this afternoon before heading off. I went out to buy some really nice cheese for Ryan. I was getting excited to meet him again. I had finally got a room at the other hotel for my last night here and would move there soon. It overlooked Durbar Square.

I went to collect some mail, confirmed my morning flight at the airline office and bought two books by Tagore: *The Broken Nest*, and *Work in Progress, Vol 4, U.S. Short Stories*.

I met Rosalie, the tall English girl again who I had seen trekking in a skirt, boots, and a brolly, and she remembered me, and my guide T.J. She looked much thinner. We admired each other, as we were both single women travelling. As I bought hot munchies I looked down and thought I had better wash my feet again. They got dirty so quickly. I traded some books back but gave the money to the boy there. I changed my remaining money to Indian rupees.

Slept with a Rat

ON FRIDAY THE 19th of October I woke in my third floor room at the Century Lodge overlooking Durbar Square. I was flat on my back and had not moved much all night. I looked to the right to my small fold-up travel clock on the bedside table and it was 6 a.m. I needed to leave pretty quickly to catch my flight to Patna. I looked out the window briefly to the Kathmandu skyline. Then I realised there was something on my feet. There was a rat the size of a cat asleep on my feet! It was very warm. It looked very comfortable.

I was clearly feeling too relaxed the night before and left the window open. This was really dumb. I usually wouldn't have left the window open because of insects. Too late now! So what to do? I carefully picked up my glasses that were next to the travel clock. I had no time to panic; I just had to do something. So I started tensing the muscles in my legs progressively down to my feet and then I was going to lift my feet and kick the rat out the window.

The rat started to wake up. It stretched a little. It looked around the room. It looked very happy. It had a good sleep. It looked at me as if I was its friend. I looked back at it. If it had been a pet cat or dog sleeping on my feet that would be different, but it was a rat! Diseases! Gross!

So immediately I tensed my feet and used them to throw it to the right across the small room. The rat hit the window frame and fell to the floor. The whole room shook a little. I flew out of bed screaming and yelling and jumping up and down. I scared the rat so much that it ran up the wall and out the window.

It was a weird feeling to have chased off my sleeping companion. Lately I had spent a lot of time on my own so strangely it had seemed for a moment like a friendly pet. I knew I was lucky it hadn't bitten me. I quickly packed my bag and headed to the airport bus. Goodbye Kathmandu.

Flew to Patna, Bus to Varanasi and Met Ryan Again

AFTER THE RAT incident I walked briskly to the Nepal Airline Office to catch the shuttle bus to the airport. On the bus I met Marlene, who wore a black harem suit and red scarf, and another lone girl with red-blond hair in plaits called Julia, from Queensland. Marlene and I had met before in South India somewhere. I bought a small bottle of whiskey at the airport. I have no idea why. Would I drink it on my own?

The clouds cleared as we took off. I could see the mountains that were the main reason I had come to Nepal. The flight was short but the bus to Varanasi was six or more hours.

On Saturday, 20th October I was in Varanasi, one of a dozen women on a woven rattan stretcher bed in a dormitory of a backpackers' called Yogi Lodge. I woke up early, went to the toilet, and then mistook Marlene's bed for mine in the dark. This created a lot of fooling around and laughing, while trying not to wake up anyone else.

When I got up later some were still asleep. There was a man reading and rattling beads along with his chanting outside this hotel. I took a rickshaw to the railway station to check about trains to Bodh Gaya and another rickshaw to the bank. I went down to the Ganges. I saw the ghats, the sets of steps leading down to the river, for the first time and close by was a small funeral pyre. It was five rupees to go out on a boat on the water opposite the ghats. They wanted to take you out early in the morning.

I had done enough wandering and researching for now. It felt like a city full of history and described as being at least 3,000 and maybe 5,000 years old. I had my bag with me and must check out lockers at the lodge, as it was getting heavy. I was cursing having too many books so stopped for a chai in a lane.

I went back to the lodge to find Marlene eating breakfast and then she went out. I then sat at a table or rested on my bed most of the day. In the early evening Ryan walked in. That was the plan in our letters but I did not know what time he might turn up.

He looked so much more relaxed than he used to, no longer so intense or overheated or angry. His face looked soft and cherubic, beautiful, with longer hair and a beard, a brown shirt, and blue pants. We looked, weighing each other up. I was full of anticipation.

We went out. He also liked my longer hair and thought I looked more relaxed too. He was not as talkative as before. It was good to see an old friend and one whom I had started out with on this trip. It was a bit like water in a desert after hanging out with strangers for so long. We talked about what we had both been doing and where we had been. He was so much calmer than I remembered. He had lost his analytical way of talking. He wasn't so critical of me.

We walked towards his hotel but then doubled back to wander more. We met Marlene, Julia, and other friends. Then Ryan and I walked on to the ghats and watched the darkness fall over the water before going back for tea at my hotel. Julia was sick in bed with diarrhoea so I gave her the homeopathic pills I had.

The plan was to meet Ryan in the morning and take a boat out on the Ganges.

I got up early. Ryan did not arrive so I went to his hotel to get him. I wondered if something was wrong or if he didn't actually want to meet up again. His reception security guard showed me where he was sleeping. He was with about six other men on rattan stretchers on a large outside balcony, the cheap sleeping place. He got up and had a quick wash and we strode out to the river. It was just dawn.

We met Marlene and Julia at one end of the steps to share a boat. Our boatman rowed out opposite the ghats with the morning's cremations on them. He slowly moved us up and down, at a distance of about fifty yards from the shore.

Out on the water I felt a profound feeling, a deep calm, and mental and emotional expansion. It was like a very deep meditation.

Being there had a very sobering and silencing effect on us all. We got off the boat and slowly walked back to the hotel. I finally remembered to give Ryan the cheese I had brought for him in Kathmandu. We shared some and it was delicious.

We went out together for a coffee and then to a short sitar recital in the area of Varanasi where there were many sitar factories and shops. Ryan was really interested in buying a sitar and learning to play it. I entertained this idea too for a few moments, as they were beautiful. Ryan went back to pack for our train trip to Bodh Gaya. We both wanted to go there.

Later I ate again at a large hotel, returned to wash my hair and sat drying it on the roof. I only had a little sleep last night so took a nap. I walked to the railway station with Marlene and bought sleeper tickets for Ryan and me to go overnight to Gaya for tonight. We stopped to see a snake charmer on the way back to our hotel.

I packed, chatted with Julia, and got my homeopathic pills back from her. She was better now. I said goodbye and gave Marlene a really big hug. She was a great person. I had to hurry up to catch the train.

It was a relaxed *cruisy* station and train ride. We were in our constantly shaking sleeper bunks all night to Gaya but it felt good to be off again.

Gaya and Bodh Gaya

On Monday the 22nd of October Ryan and I were in a hotel at Gaya where we arrived at 9 a.m. We walked up the station road and around the town. We ate a vegetarian thali of rice, dhal, and subji. We went back for a sleep and later went out for fruit, coconuts, and a lazy walk around.

It was the Lakshmi festival time. There were brightly coloured decorations around the town: flowers in oranges, yellows, and golds, plastic or real garlands all around shops, street signage and shrines to Lakshmi, the female deity of abundance. That woke us up a bit.

We went back for our bags and then headed out again. We took a rickshaw to a bus stop for the bus to Bodh Gaya. While waiting we had a chai in a café outside a bank. Since it was so hot they let us drink it inside in their air-conditioning even though Ryan was in just a singlet and white pants.

We caught a bus to Bodh Gaya, with an Eton guy who was originally from New Zealand, a French girl in a white sari with blue trim who had worked for Mother Teresa, another guy, and then a very tense Australian girl called Prue who turned up last.

Once there, we walked up and down the simple main road near the Bodhi Tree and temple area. There were many different nationality Buddhist temples and guest houses all along that road and there was a crossroad that led to a village. The temples were not very large but often quite ornate, most in walled compounds. It felt quite isolated with a low population.

The temples offered varying prices for accommodation, and activities. All the rooms were single as it was common that people came here for pilgrimages and meditation.

We chose the Burmese one for three rupees per night. There was a lecture hall there full of monks with a visiting Lama talking, but not in English. They were all really sweet people. Each room had a simple concrete slab kind of bed. The receptionist told us that if we liked we could rent a thin padded mattress to put on top of it. As it was hot weather and we were here in Bodh Gaya we thought we should try to do what the local monks did, so we slept on the concrete. I was really tired and actually slept okay. It wasn't much harder than camping in a tent on soil.

The next morning I woke up, meditated, and showered. I put on Tiger Balm to soothe my neck and back. Maybe the concrete bed was not such a good idea after all.

There was a haze of smoke coming through the bushes and trees from the morning cooking in the nearby village.

There was a herd of bullocks on the sand banks in water holes nearby. There were many baya birds and their elaborately woven nests hanging in the trees. They sang and chirped a lot so even though small they added their presence to the town. It was a peaceful place, with not many people, and lined with temples. Meditation was deeply respected and I felt good there. I felt deeply accepting of myself, and my interest in meditation.

There were some young boys there with very white teeth smiling at us and playing Frisbee. I said "Namaste" and they included us in the game.

We had a lunch and rested on the concrete beds. I used my notebook as a headrest. I was there, lying on my back, looking around my simple room at small brown sticks, ants, big and small, tiny tracings of them on the floor and up the walls. I saw trees outside that were very thin and sinewy, that had large bulbs at ground level before the trunk and branches grew out and up like a free line drawing.

I had a sleep, meditated and showered. The shower opened to the sky and I could see a soft blue through the green fern like trees.

The next morning I got up to find out that Ryan had the Indian runs. As he had stayed in Kashmir for a long time he now had not adjusted to the new food and bugs. He was also fixed in a day using the homeopathic pills.

Ryan seemed strong enough so we headed out. He seemed like a new friend rather than my old friend Ryan so I was getting to know him again. He spoke less and was doing his yoga a lot. I don't think he had been doing drugs but he was very relaxed. I missed my old friend who hid nothing. We walked to the Japanese temple, through a bazaar, up a street of houses, and across the riverbed.

We met a large, tall Dutch guy who was a practising Buddhist and lived there at the moment in Bodh Gaya. Some people stayed there for extended times. He wore the same fabric lungi that I used as a bed sheet. He also had leprosy.

As we came back from this walk, we came across a festival parade. It was like a street theatre troupe, all young men, highly decorated, with musical instruments and dancing. The dominant sound was a whistle flute with drumming in the background. The sound was clear, fresh, and distinct as out here there was no city background noise. The music travelled a long distance as they came and went. There was one tall boy dressed as a female deity, perhaps Maha Lakshmi, with white makeup on his face. He had a really elaborate dress, headdress, and jewellery. He was dancing and blessing all the others.

On Thursday the 25th of October we were still staying at the Burmese Vihar. I got up, showered, put on a blue lungi as a skirt and an orange kurta top. Ryan showed me one of the walnut wood carved chess pieces he had bought in Srinagar. It was a beautiful keepsake. He put it back in a white fluffy sock in his bag. There was another soft curved package he brought out and it was a really nice varnished wooden clock. He had used his savings to buy some really nice things but I had preferred to travel.

That morning we visited the Bodhi Tree Temple near the place where Buddha became enlightened. The original tree had died so here was a replacement. I was glad I went there and it did feel special historically. I meditated there. I didn't really feel the lightning bolt I had expected, so I thought I'd better just keep at it. From my short-term experience of meditation, I was aware that you never know when a deep or profound meditation is coming.

We also visited the Thai Temple and the Japanese Temple, where they had large, colourful, circular paintings on the ceiling. We caught the bus back to Gaya mid afternoon.

Calcutta for the Third Time and Ryan Headed Home

ON FRIDAY 26TH October we caught the night train from Gaya to Calcutta. The train kept shunting before it took off. It went on for so long all the passengers started laughing at it. It united us. It was friendly but then we all retreated to our individual bunk beds for most of the trip.

At 7 a.m. we arrived in Calcutta early and again the community of passengers made jokes about how that was a record as nothing was ever early in India. Ryan and I caught a bus into the city and had breakfast at the Woodlands.

We had wanted to stay at the Salvation Army Red Shield Guest House again but it was full. We tried a few others but no luck. So we ended up sharing a portable twin room that was one in a row of simple boxes on the actual pavement outside the Red Shield. It was just for one night.

There were tiny skinks running up and down the walls and small mice running under our beds, in and out under the walls into the street. I was a bit concerned about them but was so tired I just had to sleep. They were gone in the morning. The street noise greatly reduced overnight too. We both slept okay anyway.

I always knew I could go to a top hotel if desperate but I wanted to keep the budget constrained so I could keep travelling as long as possible. I would try and stay until December, as I had to go home and apply for college for the next year.

The next day we went to the bank to collect the six hundred dollars transferred there weeks ago. Ryan had run out of money and I was going to help him sort out his tickets home. I was happy to help him, as I didn't want him stuck there. We went to the AUS Office to arrange flights.

On Saturday the 27th of October, we stayed in the Paragon Hotel, in a large twin room. Today Ryan would go home and tomorrow I would travel on. I was a bit conflicted, but I was emboldened by the last few months of travel and still wanted to go to Rishikesh.

I said goodbye to Ryan as he headed to a shuttle for the airport. It was a simple thing. As he walked away we both looked back with a feeling of kindness. I would miss him again. I felt a lot of suppressed stifled emotions inside. This was my conflict again. Should I stick with him or keep going on my own? I was not sure what he wanted in life but he was now talking about doing less art and trying contemporary dance. I was really happy for him and he had found some peace. I felt he was not confiding in me anymore and I knew less about him than before. We had both changed.

I spent the rest of the day getting ready to travel again. I had to be brave for this next leg of my trip. I booked a train to Laksar on the Jammu Tawi Express. It was easier now in the heat and crowd as I went to the front of the queue. The system there still took time but it was okay and I got my ticket for tomorrow. Afterward to unwind I sat in the large parks at the far end of Sudder Street and sketched elephants, trees like ferns, and their seed pods.

To Laksar

ON SUNDAY THE 28th of October I woke up in the Paragon Hotel. I caught the late morning train. I talked with other passengers to pass the time. I made friends with a woman wearing a green sari. She also wore white trousers under the sari as she was trying to be modest when lying down on the train. She gave me tea.

I was reading *Through the Looking Glass* by Lewis Carroll. A piece of light classical music kept running through my mind on this train trip between reading and chatting. That amazing melody just kept running as if it was my companion.

I was happy eating the train meals. I paid the cook who came through. I bought chai at the stations, had bananas, and biscuits. The dinner I ordered didn't come so I just went to sleep hungry on my second tier bunk. I was annoyed but had no idea how to chase it up. In the morning many passengers had changed, got off and on. It was good to be tired because then I could sleep anywhere.

On Monday the 29th of October, I was still on the train to Laksar. There were many school and university boys filling the spare seats or standing. They asked me lots of questions. Was I single? Alone? How old? Where were my parents? Why? There was a friendly family nearby playing cards. They shared their food and drink with me including delicious homemade flatbreads and sweet breads.

Cracked Heads at Laksar Station

THE TRAIN ARRIVED before dawn at Laksar where I had to wait for my connection to Haridwar. It was still dark and there were crowds everywhere, on and off the train. I still had the umbrella that I had bought in Ooty. As I moved down the aisle in the train, I kept this umbrella horizontally behind me and it locked onto the seats either side of the aisle and acted as a temporary barrier. This created some space behind me. Then I would lift the umbrella barrier and move to the next two seats in the aisle.

My umbrella barrier was not respected. Everyone hated that I held them up and wanted to surge forward, but it gave me a few moments of personal space before we reached the doorway. People pushed against it and repeatedly called out "Jaldi", meaning "Quickly", I called back each time "Jaldi neh", meaning there was no rush. It translates more like "Rush was that so?" This served me well until I reached the door.

There was a crush of people pushing both on and off the train. Perhaps this was why everyone yelled "Jaldi", in order to get their blood up for what they had to fight through. I held my pack in front of my chest and then leant into the crush. It felt like I was body surfing. At times my feet were off the ground.

When I was halfway down the steps I felt a few pinches on my thigh and buttock on one side from more than one person. This got *my* blood up. I felt defensive but also outraged. I had half expected something.

As soon as my feet were on the ground, I lifted up my umbrella and swung it with all my might. I cracked it pretty strongly across a row of heads in the general direction from where the pinches had come. I heard loud cracks from the hard whacks.

Next what amazed me was that nobody reacted! Not even one person acknowledged that I had hit them. Not the men whose heads I had struck, or other men, women, or children nearby, no one reacted. The crush was the event at hand. I was of little significance or importance in this scene.

The next act and scene of this train station experience was for me to walk down the platform, over a small bridge, and down onto the next platform. I walked a gauntlet of eyes. I pretended I knew where I was going but I was looking for the ladies' toilets and waiting room, which I thought was the best place to wait for my next train. I headed for what looked to be a more central platform and area of the station rather than our side platform.

I found it by following other women. It was a relief to walk in and sign in the visitors' book which included a column where I listed which train I was waiting for. This alerted the staff to plan their time to walk women to their connecting trains. This was a great service for two rupees. I had used it before elsewhere.

I signed in and went straight to a toilet cubicle in a separate room. It was very clean with beautiful solid wood panelling. I closed the door, sat down and then laughed really hard to myself without any sound, remembering cracking heads with my umbrella. It was some kind of emotional stress release. I sat for a while then joined other ladies for company back in the waiting room to normalise myself again.

By 8:30 a.m. I was reading again. At 10 a.m. I moved to the Retiring Room, which cost about five rupees so you could lie on couches and rest.

My connection to Haridwar was soon. The tall station mistress who supervised the waiting room said she would catch my train too. We chatted, walked, and travelled together until she said goodbye after about thirty minutes into the train trip.

On Tuesday the 30th of October I was in Haridwar making my plans to go to Rishikesh. The bus to Rishikesh was only about two rupees. The Gurudev Hotel was okay last night and I discovered a new breakfast option. It was a local dish of fresh curd with tiny deep-fried dough balls mixed in it. They ran the dough across a big flat colander with holes. As the dough dropped through it into a hot wok filled with oil it made tiny dough balls. Then they were scooped up and dropped into the big bowls of fresh curd. The cook wanted to swap watches with me.

Rishikesh

RISHIKESH WAS A welcome rest from big cities. I felt okay about travelling on my own there as soon as I arrived. Many others were also travelling solo doing pilgrimages so I did not stand out anymore. Living by a fast-flowing river in the fresh air of the forest and hills was a complete delight.

I came from Haridwar to the Rishikesh bus depot. I asked about crossing the river and was offered a ride on a horse and cart for the five miles to the Ganges. I sat perched with another person on the back seat of an open tray that was covered with coarse blankets. I was itching a bit as the rugs had fleas for sure. The cart driver dropped us at a very simple stretch of riverbank. There was no bridge.

The only person there was a man who offered to take us across the river on his long thin wooden boat. He used a long pole to move the boat and would not take any money for the trip. I learnt later it was his service to others. He did it as a form of asceticism, and spiritual austerity for atonement, called Tapas. It was a peaceful few minutes crossing the quite shallow but steadily moving water.

At each stage since the bus I said that I was looking for the Maharishi T.M. Centre. Everyone knew and directed me. On the other side I asked again and was directed to the right, past shops, up the sandy beach and to follow a path into the trees. It was slow going with my bag on the sand but I made it and passed an older man with a long beard and white clothes as I arrived at the trees. There were also some men in white sitting on large boulders along the river's edge meditating. I walked into a complex of small cement and stone pod houses and larger buildings. This was a main centre for the meditation that I practiced. I asked if I was at the right place and they directed me to an office.

In the office a young T.M. Teacher spoke a little English. I asked if I could attend group meditation and also if he could recommend good accommodation. I knew they had no rooms for visitors but thought they might have advice. He came back after a few minutes with another teacher. They recommended a yoga centre guest house back down the beach to stay at. They said it was not usual to have people come for group T.M. but if I came back at 4:30 p.m. tomorrow it would be okay. I thanked them and happily headed back down the beach.

I booked in at the Ved Niketan Dhis Ashram guest house for seven rupees for a single room. I didn't have to go to the yoga classes. Each pair of rooms opened out into a shared courtyard and bathroom at the rear. The rooms were very simple concrete but really clean and quiet. It felt safe and restful. The tap water smelt fresh and was good for showering and washing clothes. Was it from the river?

I met Nick Rodgers, who told me about the post office and other places to stay: Shivanda on the other side of the river, Swarg Ashram, and then from Rishikesh, you could go to Dehradun and further. There was also a tourist bungalow on the other side. I had a list of possible accommodation for Rishikesh but this would be fine.

The next morning I got up late and did my washing. Over lunch I chatted with Brooke, a tall English girl, and Charun, an actor from Delhi. Everyone I met did some form of yoga and meditation. There was one very small Nepali man who gave out free chai.

There were various Saddhus I spoke with and most seemed very non-materialistic. There was one who would often play a flute, but another who propositioned me, saying I should come to his cave and we'll "have families." I thought that was pretty funny. There were several non-Indian Saddhus.

Rishikesh had three parts it seemed to me: a main town, then across the river a smaller town where I stayed, and then a road that led up into Himalayan foothills and mountains. As I walked up towards the mountains there were small square whitewashed houses with picket fences around them. There were bowls left outside their gates and I would see people leaving cooked rice or other food in these.

One day I was sitting on a low box seat at a tiny hut that was a grocery type of shop that sold tobacco, toothpaste, soap, Horlicks, biscuits, and so on. I looked up as someone approached. She was a very tall Germanic or European woman. My low seat may have accentuated her height. She was a lot more than six feet tall. She looked as if she may have lived in India for some time. Her hair was in long dreadlocks. She wore many strings of rudraksha beads around her neck, and layers of coarse dresses, frayed at the edges with trousers on underneath. She may have had some ash on her face or it could have been shadows that made her look ashen.

I really wanted to look at her more but thought it was rude. I took sideways glances, and pretended to be interested in the shopkeeper. When I looked back, she had vanished. I couldn't see her anywhere so it seemed as if she had disappeared.

This town was so full of compelling people and silent places.

At 4:30 p.m. I arrived at the T.M. hall. Everyone greeted me with hands together saying *Namaste*. Inside the floor was covered with thin foam mattresses covered with white-fitted sheets. It was bouncy to walk on and very comfortable to sit on. All the staff men in green uniforms sat in the back third of the space. Then there were a large number of Brahmins in white who sat in the front third of the hall. Then there were much older men in orange with long grey hair and beards who sat in a row along the far-left wall. I never saw them with their eyes opened so presumed they were doing longer meditations. I walked in and quietly sat in an open middle area. I was the only woman. A white robed Brahmin asked me if I went to reception, and I said yes.

Everyone became seated and we all closed our eyes for about twenty minutes. Then I heard someone move to the low stage at the front. He gently rang a small bell, softly said, "Jai Guru Dev" and then sang a brief chant in Sanskrit. It was a gentle way to finish. After two or three minutes I opened my eyes. I saw him sitting next to a picture of Guru Dev (Maharishi's teacher) displayed on a small table. That meditation was an extremely awake one with what seemed to be unbounded subtly ringing silence with very few thoughts. I felt the effect of that silent, still hall in my mind and body for many hours afterwards.

All the staff in green left when I did. The others continued. I felt really super at ease there as we were connected though T.M. but everyone was so sweet and caring. I really enjoyed going there, felt accepted and very safe. I forgot I was the only woman almost immediately.

I went each afternoon at the same time. The teachers had become used to looking out for me so it felt as if I had a few friends there. One day I arrived and they said it was a public holiday so they didn't usually hold the group meditation. I must have looked disappointed as they all spoke between themselves and then sent around a message that they would have it anyway.

They let me join a tour of Maharishi's house there one day and I was able to have a good look around. While there wasn't much English spoken, it felt very meaningful to hear some things about the beginnings of T.M. being told to the group. I saw a photo hanging above a picture rail, which had Guru Dev, seated in the middle. He had six men seated either side of him; they were Saddhus and Brahmacharis. One of them was Maharishi and another was the bald man in whose yoga centre I was staying.

When I meditated there, I experienced a huge contrast to doing it on my own. There was not a sense of settling down and then surfacing again at the end. There was instead a clear, strong sense of being very calm, very still, and that it was a continuum with eyes opened or eyes closed. In that hall both in and out of meditation I had very few thoughts in my mind, felt very relaxed, and happy.

One day there, I had a distinct thought in meditation that was quite visual. It came for a moment and was then gone, but

I cannot forget it. It was a mental picture of a small clear bubble that contained within it everything I would do in my life. It was a brilliant, rapid movie. The knowledge of what it was came with it. This is my best description of it. The group meditations there were unforgettable yet extremely simple at the same time.

I also met a T.M. teacher couple who were staying at the same ashram guest house. They told me no one could go up to the T.M. Centre as it was just for Indians. But I had, and I was going again tomorrow. They were a bit surprised and couldn't work it out. I thought it maybe was because I was quite harmless and they could see that.

That couple gave me some *prasad* or blessed food from a saint they had visited in the caves. It was a plastic bag full of delicious, still warm, potatoes fried in ghee, salt, mustard seeds, and curry leaves. We all ate it up. They were leaving soon so I promised to write to them if Maharishi came here to Rishikesh. I liked the idea that Maharishi did not want people to worship him as they had told me.

At the guest house I also met a Spanish guy, a very young Dutch guy who was volunteering with a charity group, a Palestinian guy, a Costa Rican girl, and a Swedish guy who helped with his cigarette lighter at different times to light the candle in my room since I had no matches. I enjoyed all the people there.

I remembered that swimming in the Ganges River in Rishikesh was a traditional spiritual and cultural practice. I felt it was quite poetic and planned to do it but was a shy and gauche tourist so I had to think how to do this carefully.

So the next day I carried a bag full of washing and walked for about an hour on the road heading up towards the mountains behind Rishikesh. There were less and less people walking until there was no-one else in sight. It became peaceful only hearing the padding of my slip-on shoes on the road but I was still also anxious about being a lone woman.

The mountain was on my right side. On my left I was looking for somewhere safe and private to go down onto the banks of the river. I hoped for a swim where the river was not too wild and easy to get in and out of. I realised having a swim in my bikini, on my own, might be provocative and was not safe. So I worked hard to find a completely private place where no one would see me. And I did find a place.

Behind extensive bushes I looked down to the river and was able to climb over large boulders that hid the area from the road. Once there, I could sit in the sun on my own riverbed space protected from the wind and eyes. I could lie down and sunbathe, as I had been unable to do at many beach spots while travelling. So I took off my clothes down to my bathers and emptied the washing out of my bag. I washed them all with a bar of soap in the river and then hung them on smaller rocks and bushes to dry.

The Ganges here opened up into a wide, dark green, rapidly flowing river. I could barely make out the details of a woman washing clothes on the opposite bank. While the clothes dried, I took my chance for a swim. I had chosen this area also because it had a couple of huge boulders that created a calm pool of water behind them. I stepped in slowly to check its sandy bottom. It was stable enough and the water was warm. I had really lucked out. I really enjoyed this and dunked my head a few times completely under as I had seen Saddhus and pilgrims do.

At that moment in the freedom of swimming in a quiet pool that was part of that fiercely wild and stunningly beautiful river I was moved. I cherished these few minutes of freedom, swimming in this water, but more than that I appreciated the simple things in life that underlie all the complexities. It was symbolic of accomplishing something. I barely understood what I was going through. Life can be hard but it can also be simple and I was looking for some kind of freedom and guts to work with going forward.

I then walked back as I wanted to get to the meditation at 4:30.

The teachers there told me that Maharishi would be in Delhi for twenty days. They didn't know if he would come here but they were all cleaning anyhow. They said I could go to Delhi and can come back later to their group meditations if I liked.

So what to do? I had to do something. I could not stay here forever and I had a life to go back to. I was going to become a teacher and build a life. I wondered if I would be bored? I really wanted to keep my art going too. This year had been so stimulating, yet peaceful and free, but my money would run out. I would travel again later on. It was too romantic and fanciful to stay here. Or I could do nothing.

I decided to go to Delhi. I would then work out my next step. I was talking with the reception guy about keeping a diary and he was telling me why they were no good. He liked to be in the present moment. He invited me to the room where some chanting will begin. He said he would fix my room light, when the electricity came back on, if I wanted to stay.

I felt the need to go to Delhi but also the usual trepidation in heading off to a new place as a jump to uncertainty. A big butterfly swooped out the door with me as I left and fluttered away. As I walked to the shops a bike rider who passed close by startled me out of my overthinking with his *ding-dong, ding-dong* and horn.

I took a bus to Haridwar and another to Delhi. There was a Rajneesh follower called Aaron on both buses so we talked a bit. I asked him a lot about his beliefs. He was wearing an orange baggy Indian suit, had knotted manic hair, beads, and a picture of his guru around his neck. He seemed a nice person. He was French and an independent schoolteacher with a son.

Delhi

Aaron knew about a guest house in central Delhi very close to Connaught Circle and a good supermarket for shopping. So we went there. It was a large house divided into small rooms and I got a room for eight rupees per night.

A large friendly Sikh man ran the guest house. He wore white trousers and a white singlet, with his hair and beard in a net. He had family including a young boy in jeans and t-shirt. I think he was friendly as a strategy to know what everyone was up to. He was very streetwise and I felt protected by that.

We discussed my trip. What to do next? Was I interested in sleeping, travelling, walking, or swimming? My interest was artwork. His could be music. We agreed you could also do nothing in life. I thought we were both joking.

Later I was walking, walking, walking, and exploring Delhi. I visited an ancient temple nearby in Janpath Lane. The people there described it as two thousand five hundred years old. It had a statue, related to Shiva, of the *eyes of a god* embedded in a big round orange and red sculpture.

While in Delhi I went to a Bharatanatyam performance by a renowned woman, called *Dances of India*, at the Jhankar Theatre, Mandi House. It was stunning in complexity and the costumes were extremely beautiful silks. She and all the dancers must be incredibly fit and devoted to this art.

I kept to myself at the guest house, went to bed early, wrote in my diary, and read letters. In Delhi I had new letters from Ryan, my youngest sister, and my Mum. Ryan wrote that he thought all desire was illusion and a tighter bind on the wheel of life. One day I had also walked to the Tourist Camp and picked up Ryan's tent, blue lungi, and other items he had stored there and posted them home to him. I took a Harley Davidson taxi back, which was fun.

The next morning after a few practical errands I went to a circus with Aaron that included some acrobats, clowns and several lions doing tricks when a whip was cracked in the central caged area of the big tent. One large old female lion urinated towards the sparse audience and luckily it missed most and us. We also had a great lunch in a downstairs bazaar on the way.

As we were walking back through some backstreets, I found a poster about a Rajneesh Meditation Weekend, which he thought he would go to.

Jaipur

THE FOLLOWING DAY I took the five or six hour bus to Jaipur. Anna and Tim wanted to bypass Rajasthan; so on our way south earlier in the year I had missed it. Now I made the effort to come back. I carried water, bananas, and packets of biscuits, and snacked all day on vendor food I bought from my window at bus stops along the way. I had chai, peanuts boiled with their shells on and served in a cone of rolled newspaper, and chapattis.

I booked in to a hotel in Jaipur where Marlene and Julia from Varanasi were already staying. We had planned to meet up. I walked around town, saw the fort on a hilltop nearby, had a swim and rested by the pool at our hotel. It was an above-ground, roughly made concrete and brick pool with steps up to get in. Inside it was tiled and pretty neat. I had a sore ear so I kept my head out of the water. Later I went to an ear specialist for twenty rupees and got some capsules for about ten rupees. I had an ear infection.

That evening I met up with Julia and another Queenslander Mason. Then Marlene, who was still and always wearing black with a red scarf, arrived too. Julia gave us all her contact details and told us about all the things she would do if we visit her at

Cooly, Coolangatta. She had long blond hair and wore short sundresses with thin tie straps. She spoke loudly and stood out in a crowd there in India. Some men had thrown metals filings on her bare shoulders at the market here in Jaipur but she was unapologetically being herself.

The next day we all went to the Old Palace and the Amber Palace. I loved the Pink City, named after the colour of its buildings. The town was planned and built by a Raja in the 1700s following the ancient principles of Vastu. Today I felt as if I didn't have my mind anymore. Maybe it was the ear infection. I would be happy to throw away my diaries, I was writing rubbish. I was thinking about going to a small place for two weeks after Delhi, maybe Sarnath.

I wrote to Shanti in Pondicherry.

Back to Delhi

I TRAVELLED BACK to Delhi. No more diaries. I was getting tired of writing my daily notes. Writing when I only want in rather than just doing it habitually. No more reading philosophy since before Rishikesh and it was great. I have my mind back. I went back to the same guest house as before but they were full so he could only offer me the veranda room until someone left.

The next morning I woke up and I felt okay but when I went to the toilet I had red urine and white stools. My eyes were yellow and I had no appetite. I headed off to the nearby hospital to find a doctor. I was glad I was in a big city for this. It was serious but I tried not to worry. Maybe this would force me to go home. I was solution orientated rather than letting myself freak out.

I stood in a line of about twenty people outside the hospital and a doctor looked out and signalled to me to come to him. I didn't like to jump the queue but he insisted.

He said I had jaundice and after hearing about my travelling said it was probably hepatitis from bad drinking water. He also said that the incubation time was three weeks so in thinking about where I was then I remembered a waiter with yellow eyes in Kathmandu. He gave me a diet to stick to: high protein and rice, Vitamin B supplement, three eggs per day, curd, fish, chicken, jam, sweet biscuits, fruit juice, lemon water, and glucose powder drinks. He said that was all you did to get better but he wanted to keep an eye on me. I had to visit him every two days at his home surgery. I had to note my symptoms every day and give him a call if I got worse. He gave me his card. He wanted me to find better accommodation and just sleep and rest until the symptoms reverted back to reasonably normal.

The next day the symptoms were still similar but I found another hotel. I got a supply of what I needed from the chemist. I didn't feel too anxious about it all as the main symptom I had was fatigue and that wasn't slowing me down too much. I had no surplus energy to worry possibly. I thought I had found a really competent doctor so I would rest and follow all his advice.

At my new hotel the receptionist noticed my yellow skin but I had a note from the doctor saying I was not contagious and they should accept me.

I did visit him every two days at his home office. I would catch a tuk-tuk or taxi there and back. He took me into his living room for a chat over a cup of tea, served in a teacup and saucer. It was a warm family brick home with a separate door for his office. The living room had a TV and sideboard with doilies and vases on it. One time he and his family had just finished eggs, bacon, and toast for breakfast. It was all very middle class and familiar.

After about a week I felt pretty good again. Energy levels were back and all the main symptoms were gone. I slept a lot so was not too lonely even though it was a bit boring being there. I began thinking about heading home. It was a bit disappointing but I had been to all the Indian places that I had really wanted to go.

On the 17th of November I changed a few traveller's cheques, and confirmed my air tickets from Delhi to Calcutta, then Calcutta to Bangkok, where I had to wait a week for my connection to Sydney and Melbourne.

Bangkok

Bangkok was very crowded. I shared a room with a few guys I met at the AUS Office there. The receptionist encouraged us to stick together and advised us of a place to stay. There were four guys, a French, an American, and two Germans. We visited temples, markets, and sights together for a few days.

They took me to a really intense Bangkok nightclub. Everyone was very highly made-up, bejewelled and over-dressed. The French and American guys were my bodyguards for the night. We squeezed through the crush in the club getting many propositions. They sat me in a corner and sat either side of me. They backed me up during an attempted bag snatch on a bus another day.

Later on at the AUS Office in Bangkok, I met Alistair; the Melbourne journalist who I'd spent time with earlier in Kathmandu with his partner Louise. He was also travelling home while she had already gone back. I shared the twin hotel room he already had. It was great to be with an Australian again, to be able to speak rapidly and freely. Alistair was a pragmatist, intensely interested in politics and world news. The room was pretty basic with two single beds, side tables, a coffee table and a couple of armchairs. There were black metal bars on the windows and a strong door with a metal grid door too.

Both his bedside table and the coffee table were covered in empty, small bar fridge sized alcohol bottles. There were a few glasses and a couple of empty large bottles of spirits too. I thought he drank too much but we didn't discuss it.

After a couple of days I was able to get my Qantas flight home. On the flight the stewards and the food seemed so *larger-than-life* Australian, their accents seemed broad, and they seemed way too happy. It was weird to leave India. Perhaps it had become a second home. I had got quite used to being there. I felt I was back in Australia as soon as I got on the plane. I had mixed emotions leaving India but was getting excited to go home now. I had no regrets. I had given it a good go and I was still alive!

This is where the diary ended.

Melbourne

I ARRIVED BACK in Melbourne early one morning in the first week of December, with three hundred dollars in unused traveller's cheques. I had been away for about seven months. I got on an airport shuttle bus and experienced more culture shock on that ride than anywhere else during the whole trip. I was the only person on the full-sized bus so moved up to the front and chatted with the driver. There was no one on the streets, no one walking, no one living rough, and barely any traffic. I kept asking the driver, "Where is everyone?"

I caught a train to my parents' home, but I had not told anyone I was coming. As I walked down our street I met my Dad walking up to the shops to buy a newspaper and milk. He reacted with a big shudder when he saw me and broke into a big smile. We kissed and hugged.

He took my bag, swung it over his shoulder and said, "Come with me." As we called in to shops, he would say, "This is my daughter, she has just come back from India." Dad and I really enjoyed that walk, beginning to reconnect and then arriving home to surprise Mum together.

And Then

WHAT HAD I gotten out of my trip? Was I still restless? Had I filled my existential vacuum? I have no idea how I am to answer these questions as I do not remember but looking back there were substantial knock-on effects.

In February 1980 at the orientation day for my education studies, my work and recent travel experiences were noted. I was asked to join the cohort to work in the alternative and independent community school stream. I did my teaching round experience all over Melbourne in diverse community schools. The next year I worked one full-time term in a regular technical school but I preferred relief teaching in many schools: in the 1980s and 1990s in Melbourne, in the late 1990s and 2000s in Perth, and when back in Melbourne again with the last being in 2009. This allowed me to pursue other interests: T.M., my art practice, and travel. I didn't go back to competitive athletics. I did meet Maharishi on subsequent trips. I do still meditate every day.

What I do remember is that we began our travel full of excitement and optimism. There were about twenty friends and family who saw us off at the airport. On the plane out of Melbourne we were talking really fast, full of adrenalin, sitting forward and upright in our seats. I was travelling with two friends who I had met through art school. They were not close friends, but they were good friends; people to share things with and work things out with, but perhaps not to confide in. But as this didn't last, I learnt to rely on myself and although very anxious at times, I had to focus and work things through.

At that time, I had a head full of world philosophies and had been reading widely for the last two or three years due to discovering the Theosophical Society Library in Melbourne. I would borrow armloads of books from diverse histories to psychology to philosophy and devour the lot.

I might have seemed like a hippie, as I went to art school and did this trip. I did sometimes wear kurta tops, sit in lotus, have long hair, listen to Jimi Hendrix and Janis Joplin and practice T.M., but I came later. In 1979 it really was the very end of the *hippie trail*.

The truth was that for this trip I cut my hair short, and returned after it still not a hippie, not an alcoholic or drug addict, still single, and still a virgin. I faked it a lot when drugs were passed around as I had asthma. I was not wild, I was game and I was lucky. This was the first of several trips to India, travelling or living there for work, while the last was in 2011 when I was researching Vastu principles of architecture for some postgraduate study.

About twenty years ago I met a woman in Australia who had also been in Srinagar in 1979. We realised we had been there on different houseboats at the same time. She mentioned that she had met Ryan and they had a short relationship during the time I travelled south. Ryan never mentioned this. Had this been part of why he was so calm and changed when we met again?

Ryan was an important friend for me but as it turned out only temporarily. He moved interstate after this trip, and passed away in his thirties. Vale Ryan.

So the diary ended. I could have edited it to be a creative fiction with a *beginning, middle, and end*. Ryan and I were possibly in love, fell out of it, got back together and found it was real. I wouldn't do that to you. Or my editing might have produced a *coming of age* resilience and *understanding more things about life* book. I couldn't do that to you or me.

1979 was pivotal for me. It was defining. It was a year of walking, diverse experiences, people and meditation. Reading my diary again after so many years unlocked memories of many places and moments. There is no conclusion. There was no conclusion. Life was open-ended in every direction. Life is open-ended in every direction, undefined, imprecise, and at times compelling.

www.ingramcontent.com/pod-product-compliance
Lightning Source LLC
Chambersburg PA
CBHW062046290426
44109CB00027B/2747